A HISTORY OF

VALENTINES

You'll give your shins the cold, little dame,
Your attitude's so bold—fie, for shame!
Like a spider in its net, sitting there,
You make one blush, and yet stand and stare.

Frontis. The pert little glamor girl of the 1840's.

A HISTORY OF

VALENTINES

RUTH WEBB LEE

THE STUDIO PUBLICATIONS, INC.
in association with
THOMAS Y. CROWELL COMPANY
New York and London

ST. VALENTINE,
PATRON SAINT OF LOVERS

COPYRIGHT 1952 BY
THE STUDIO PUBLICATIONS, INC.

MANUFACTURED IN THE UNITED STATES OF AMERICA

Designed by Betty R. Binns

LIBRARY OF CONGRESS CARD NO. 52–7866

1 2 3 4 5 6 7 8 9 10

ACKNOWLEDGMENTS

WRITING ABOUT VALENTINES HAS proved to be a most entertaining diversion, after spending more than twenty years doing books devoted to various types of early American glass. It has not been an easy task to attempt a classification of the varied kinds of valentines produced by so many concerns, both here and in England, over several centuries. Considering the fact that the late Jonathan King of London, a valentine manufacturer, accumulated about eight tons of them, will give the reader an idea of the enormity of the undertaking facing any researcher into the subject. A really comprehensive book would need to be monumental. The best the author could hope to accomplish was to paint a bird's-eye view of the history and progress, from Roman times until the present, of valentine styles and the processes by which they were made. It is hoped that the only sins will be those of omission, which must be expected of a pioneer book.

The compilation of this volume has been made lighter by the kind assistance of good friends. Their interest never waned, perhaps because there is at least a little sentiment in all of us, even though it may be buried deeper during these troubled times.

I am greatly indebted to Mr. and Mrs. Charles Albert Read of Salem, Massachusetts. Being ardent collectors, as well as students, of valentines, they recognized many of the problems facing me and helped in many invaluable ways. Mere words cannot always express the depth of one's appreciation. Clarence Brigham, Director of the American Antiquarian Society in Worcester, Massachusetts, was always most courteous in extending the facilities of that noble institution, including the use of their large collection of valentines and vast store of valuable documents. Mr. Brigham's efficient staff also earned my eternal gratitude. Arthur G. Waite, who has been with the Antiquarian Society for some thirty-five years, spent hours doing a report of the final days of the George C. Whitney Company, which is of considerable value as an authentic record.

Esther B. Mooney, of Norcross, New York, went far beyond the call of duty in her kindly assistance. It was the first time in my experience with some ten book titles, which include thousands of illustrations, that anyone ever arranged photographs for me. It is a time-consuming task and one which requires an endless amount of patience. Her helping hand hastened the conclusion of this book, for which I shall always be grateful. Having access to the Norcross collection, which is probably the most comprehensive in our country today, was priceless in itself.

The Museum of the City of New York was most kind in allowing me the use of any specimens in their collection, some of which are illustrated, and I regret my inability to have spent more time with them. Mrs. Harry Shaw Newman kindly permitted me to photograph any of her rare hand-made valentines, as did Mrs. K. Gregory, also of New York. Examples from both their collections are shown.

Mrs. W. S. Curtis of Youngstown, Ohio, who has collected many beautiful valentines, kindly sent me a number of photographs covering some of her most interesting items, but unfortunately my book was completed before they arrived. However, it was possible to add three, which will be found among the illustrations.

I am also indebted to S. Q. Shannon, of the National Association of Greeting Card Publishers, for his kindly interest, and to *People and Places* magazine for a photograph.

C O N T E N T S

PART ONE

I

ST. VALENTINE

DEAR TO THE HEARTS of Americans are three patron saints: St. Nicholas of yuletide fame, beloved by children; St. Patrick, beloved by our Irish-American patriots; and St. Valentine, patron saint of lovers.

The history of St. Valentine, "Valentinus," and the origin of the custom of celebrating February 14 as St. Valentine's Day has been nearly lost in antiquity, but it is possible to piece the legend together supported by a number of authenticated facts.

Probably the first representation of St. Valentine to appear in a printed book is the one illustrated on page 4—from *The Nuremberg Chronicle*. the great "picture book" of the fifteenth century. Written first in Latin by Hartmann Schedel and translated into German six months later, this work purported to be a history of the world from its creation until 1493. By actual count, the *Chronicle* contains 645 woodcuts for 1809 different subjects. The artists responsible for the woodcuts are Wohlgemuth, the teacher of Albrecht Dürer, and his stepson, Pleydenwurff. The book was financed by two wealthy Nuremberg patricians and printed by Nuremberg's greatest printer, Anton Koberger.

The charm of *The Nuremberg Chronicle* lies in the fact that it gives us an actual glimpse of daily life as it existed some five centuries ago, for the artists portray all peoples and places as similar to those of Nuremberg at the end of the fifteenth century.

The representation of St. Valentine bearing his martyr's palm, shown here in plate 1, is taken from the first edition of the *Chronicle*, published in Nuremberg in July 1493. The accompanying text mentions that he was a Roman priest and gives a brief account of his martyrdom during the days of Claudius II. His feast date is given as March 16, but nothing is said of his role as patron of lovers. When the German edition of the *Chronicle* appeared in December 1493, it was virtually the same account, but fixed the feast day as February 14.

Valentinus was said to have performed valiant service in assisting Christian martyrs during their persecution under Emperor Claudius II in Rome. Giving aid and comfort to Christians at that time was looked upon

3

Plate 1.   St. Valentinus.

as a crime, accordingly Valentinus was arrested and imprisoned for it.

A year later he was taken before the emperor, whom he tried to convert to Christianity. The Roman ruler was so impressed by the priest's dignity that he attempted to save Valentinus by in turn trying to convert him to the Roman gods. "What thing is that which I have heard of thee, Valentinus?" he asked. "Why wilt thou not abide in amity and worship the idols and renounce the vain opinion of thy creance?"

Valentinus courageously, but very injudiciously replied, "I say of thy gods none other thing but that they were men mortal and merchant and full of ordure and evil."

For allowing valor to overcome discretion, Valentinus was immediately condemned, first to be beaten with clubs, then stoned, and finally to be beheaded outside the Flaminian Gate. Legend has it that the priest, while waiting execution, formed a friendship with the blind daughter of

4

his jailor,[1] whose sight he was able to restore. Doubtless saddened by his fate, he wrote a farewell message to her on the eve of his death and signed it, "From your Valentine." If true, then it was the origin of an expression which has been used millions of times over the centuries. The good priest could never know that his note of farewell would be perpetuated in the hearts of lovers, on the anniversary of his death. Thereafter, the Flaminian Gate where he was executed was known as Porta Valentini, later being renamed Porta Popolo. He was buried in what is now the Church of Praxedes in Rome, where it is said that a pink almond tree blossomed near his grave, a symbol of abiding love.

Some skeptics have thought that there is no connection whatever between the holy man of the third century and the custom of exchanging lace-paper conceits popularly known as valentines, beyond the fact that the saint died on the fourteenth day of February. They seem, however, to be somewhat in error.

One interpretation [2] of the connection between the saint and the lover's feast concerns a custom sometimes spoken of as existing among the ancient Romans, of celebrating a festival on the fourteenth of February in honor of their goddess, Juno Regina. At this feast it was the practice for boys to draw by lot the names of girls, who were their partners in the celebration.

It has been said that the early Christian pastors desired to abolish what they termed "this lewd custom of the heathen." But knowing it would be impossible to eradicate it immediately, they proceeded to give it a Christian touch by substituting the names of saints for the names of girls. Thus in the mutation of time the custom has grown which now takes the form of valentines.

The date of the beheading of St. Valentine is given as February 14, of the year 270.[3] His martyrdom would seem to have no relationship whatever with the exchanging of valentines, but there is a direct, though accidental link, for his death occurred at the time of year when the holiday spirit was much in evidence. It was the eve of the ancient feast of the Lupercalia, when the Romans habitually preserved the memory of an ancient rural god, Faunus. It is not difficult to imagine that the public beheading of Valentinus, the Christian, became a natural part of the pagan celebration of the Lupercalia.

Faunus was the god of animal life, patron of husbandry, hunting, and herding, as well as guardian of the secret lore of nature. On the Palatine

[1] The jailor was Asterius, one of the Emperor's lieutenants, according to Alfonso Villiegas in his *Lives of Saints.* Asterius and his family were converted to Christianity by St. Valentine, and as a result were all condemned to death by Claudius II.

[2] Dr. Butler's *Lives of the Saints.*

[3] According to Alfonso Villiegas in *Lives of Saints,* written in Spanish A.D. 1630 and translated into Italian, and English, St. Valentine was beheaded A.D. 271.

Hill was a cave sacred to him, on which, according to legend, Romulus and Remus had been suckled by the she-wolf. This cave was called the Lupercal, probably from that incident—the Latin word "lupus" meaning wolf.

On February 15, at the door of this cave, the priests of Lupercus sacrificed a goat and a dog. With the blood-stained knife, the officiating priest would then touch two selected young men on their foreheads, wiping the blood off with wool dipped in milk. Whereupon, according to the ritual, the two young men were required to laugh out loud. At this point, the priests of Lupercus, known as Luperci, naked except for a goat skin about their loins, made a circuit of the Palatine Hill, waving strips of skin from the freshly slaughtered goats. Any woman whom they encountered they struck upon the palms of the hands with these thongs, and it was supposed that this practice would produce fertility.

The name of these thongs was februa, and the ritual itself was called

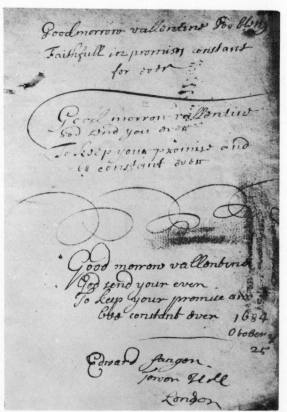

Plate 2.

St. Valentine greeting, dated October 25, 1684.

6

the februatio, whence, of course, was finally derived our month February.

It was not so many years after the death of Valentinus that Christianity spread over all Rome, and the wise Christian priests sublimated popular pagan festivals, making them into Christian feasts. Thus it seems possible that the feast of Lupercalia became associated at this time with St. Valentine.

Some authorities believe that the word "valentine" came from the Norman word "Galatin," meaning a gallant, or lover. Despite those who may scoff at the many legends, the fact remains that the ancient Roman custom of young men and maidens drawing names for their mates was introduced into England, where it was carried on for many centuries, and more often than not, ended in marriage. Also significant is the fact that the old English poet John Lydgate, who died in 1450, spoke of the "custome of Seynte Valentine" as a "religioun."

In 1614 the poet Donne wrote in his epithalamium on the marriage of Princess Elizabeth to Frederick, Count Palatine of the Rhine, which took place on St. Valentine's Day:

> "Hail, Bishop Valentine! Whose day this is;
>   All the air is thy diocese,
>   And all the chirping choristers
>   And other birds thy parishoners."

So the ancient custom of observing St. Valentine's Day stems from the early Romans but over the centuries has become imbued with Anglo-Saxon sentiment. The first written message using St. Valentine's name known in this country, though of English origin, is illustrated in plate 2. Written three times, it finally evolved into the following:

> "Good morrow Vallentine,
>   God send you ever
>   To keep your promise and
>   bee constant ever." (dated) 1684
>   October 25.
>   (signed) Edward Sangon,
>   Tower Hill
>   London.

II

AMERICAN HANDMADE VALENTINES

1740 — 1840

IT IS ALWAYS INTERESTING to a collector to trace the origin of a custom that produced the articles he collects and to reflect upon the contemporary times and habits. In the case of valentines, the earliest were entirely handmade and many of them are rare enough so that they are virtually museum pieces today. In this modern day it is difficult to transport our thoughts backward to the period prior to the American Revolution to picture for the moment their mode of living. At that time, the youth of our country had ample leisure to create handmade valentines, for there were no movies, radio, television, trains, nor automobiles for distraction. There was more time for love and sentiment and these were in abundance, especially come February 14!

It may also be noted that valentines were posted by hand, usually deposited on the lady's doorstep. There were no envelopes then as we know them today. The valentines were folded and sealed with wax. Those that were despatched by stage coach might be enclosed in another wrapper but they were still sealed with a small dab of wax, generally red in color. It was not until 1845 that uniform postage rates were established in this country. Mail was prepaid, and the postal official stamped the envelope, the mark seen most often being a darkish-red irregular circle enclosing a "Paid 5" in the center. To collectors, certain of these old envelopes are actually more valuable than the valentines themselves, especially when they carry local or private postage stamps.

The history of the valentine in this country appears to have begun during the middle of the eighteenth century. The early pieces were often simple, yet artistic in style, and for the most part displayed excellent taste in design. Not as much may be said for many of the accompanying verses, which were also usually "homemade."

These early valentines were laboriously wrought by various processes from water color to pen work, to "pin pricks" and "cutouts," beautifully colored. There were also the rebuses, acrostics, and other styles of puzzles, or cryptograms. An excellent example of an acrostic may be seen on plate 3. It is one of the best eighteenth-century handmade valentines of this

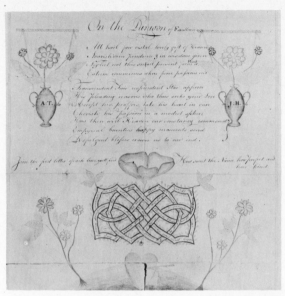

Plate 3. American handmade acrostic.

type, probably executed about 1760, in or around Philadelphia. Many, many hours must have been devoted by the swain who not only designed, painted the *magnum opus* and composed the verses, but further embellished his work of art by a so-called "endless knot of love," which carries running lines concerning his blissful state, winding throughout. The poem is titled "On the Paragon of Excellence." Apparently his original intent was not to go beyond "Paragon," but he finally crowded in "of Excellence"! Across the center of this valentine is written, "Join the first letter of each line you'll find, How sweet the name, how perfect and how kind." The poem follows:

> "All hail fair vestal, lovely gift of heaven,
> Nourished in prudence and in wisdom given.
> Neglect not this small present from a friend,
> Esteem commences where fierce passions end.
>
> Transcendent Fair resplendent star approve
> His pleading reasons who thus seeks your love,
> Accept his proffers, take his heart in care.
> Cherish his passion in a modest sphere.
> How then will heaven our constancy commend.
> Empyreal bounties happy moments send,
> Refulgent blisses crown us to our end."

9

It will be noted that the first letter of each line finally add up to the name of his ladylove, Anne Thacher.

Not infrequently will the collector encounter a rare item, which may or may not be a valentine, for in the early days, love tokens in one form or another were frequently presented to loved ones. It is sometimes difficult to be absolutely certain when an object is truly a valentine. Plate 4 presents this problem, though in this instance the handmade, gaily colored circle is probably a valentine. The verse reads: "May our hearts like these forever be, As closely bound in unity." The particular interest in this piece, aside from its early associations and general attractiveness, is the edge, which has a narrow silk tape binding, carefully and neatly sewn to the paper. So their love is bound!

The Pennsylvania-German valentine on plate 5 was sent by "Philipp" to his loved one, apparently in Lancaster, Pennsylvania, from Betschdorf, as this was purchased in Lancaster some years ago. The style of decoration is typically Pennsylvania-German in character. Translated, it reads:

"God and the Trinity thought up the institution of marriage. He also told me the oath which I give you today, my birdie. If you will become my wife, I will be faithful and exercise pious duties, that good fortune and peace will grow and besides this, our house and wealth will profit by the work which we do. This do I write to you, beloved treasure, your faithful Philipp, in the year 1753."

Plate 4.

Handmade
valentine.

10

Plate 5.

Pennsylvania-German valentine, dated 1753.

It is amazing that this treasure from Philipp's hand has survived in such perfect condition after nearly two hundred years. Fortunate indeed is the collector who adds a rarity of such an early date as this one to his collection, and in such a perfect state of preservation.

Among the most interesting, as well as quaint, of the really old valentines, is the rebus. Plate 6 pictures one open, and plate 7 shows both sides when folded properly. The puzzle consists in refolding one of these valentines, once it has been opened. The verses in this type are usually, though not always, numbered. Numbering them was practically a necessity, and at that, the recipient had a merry time twisting it this way and that before she could decipher the message from her suitor. Generally, though not always, the lines were simple and to the point. The rebus illustrated on plate 6 is typical of many and the numbered lines read as follows:

1. You are the girl and only maid,
   Who has my tender heart betrayed.
2. Tis you and only you can cure
   The wracking pain that I endure.
3. If you refuse to be my wife
   It will bereave me of my life
4. Pale death at last must be my friend
   And bring my sorrows to an end.

11

The circular ornament in the center also carries an inscription around it, thus: "This ring is round, and has no end, So is my love to you my friend."

The rather masculine appearing angels adorning two corners of this valentine, if one may call them angels, are so formidable in appearance that they may well have frightened the young miss into accepting her suitor in a hurry. Curiously, the two lower corners carry the patriotic figure of a man wearing a blue coat and red and white striped trousers. In one view he is holding a scroll, and in the other, optimistically leading a young lady over the waves toward a ship, which displays a large American flag. Thus, the birthplace of this rare valentine is unmistakable.

The verses on the two sides of the folded rebus are so typical of many (plate 7) that they are quoted. The one having the heart in the center reads:

> "The heart that you do now behold,
> Will break when you these lines unfold,
> Even so, my heart with lovesick pain,
> Sore wounded is and breaks in twain."

Plate 6. Handmade valentine, known as a rebus.

Plate 7.

Front and reverse of rebus, when folded.

The quatrain on the other side is more hopeful. It goes as follows:

> "On the outside sweet turtle dove,
> I write the passions of my love,
> No power of envy can pretend
> To say that I false lines have penned."

Any rebus is extremely rare today, particularly in anything approaching good condition. The old paper is thick and rather brittle, so that folding and unfolding over the years has contributed little toward its preservation.

Collection of Mrs. Harry Shaw Newman

Plate 8. American handmade rebus.

Valentine Writers [1] from England were known in this country as early as 1723, which must account for some of the rebuses carrying identical verses. However, in the example of a more elaborate valentine of this sort, such as that illustrated in plate 8, the verse could hardly have been copied from a book, considering the spelling. He speaks of "Pail death at last" this line appearing beneath the skeleton in the upper-left corner,

[1] Booklets devoted to verses for use in handmade valentines.

while "It will bereeve me" occurs under the chubby figure at the lower left. His "hearts are in the right place," but his spelling was evidently neglected!

The rebus shown in plate 9 is particularly interesting because it was written and hand painted during the period when young men were still drawing lots for their sweethearts. It also proved the contention that this custom continued for many years in this country, just as it did for centuries in England and Scotland. Let us examine the verses, which are numbered.

Norcross, New York

Plate 9. American handmade rebus.

1 If you do these lines refuse,
   Pray burn the same and me excuse.
2 You are the same I drew last year,
   It was because I lov'd you dear.
3 Nor do I expect on earth to find,
   Not one like you to please my mind.
4 When I did draw my valentine,
   It was my fortune you to find.

15

5　On the 14th of February
　　We were dispos'd to be merry.
6　Our lots we cast and, thus I drew,
　　Kind fortune says it must be you.
7　Sure as the grapes hang on the vine,
　　So sure you are my valentine.
8　And in you I do hope to find,
　　On(e) agreeable to my mind.

The youth who designed this valentine was not only an artist but a penman extraordinary. His lettering is so finely executed as to give the appearance of printing. In days gone by penmanship was indeed a cultivated art.

An exquisite example of the cutout, which is also in the nature of a rebus, may be seen in plate 10. The workmanship is so delicate and the paper so fragile that the whole has been mounted against a background of very fine muslin, in order to preserve it. The verses in many of these ancient valentines bear repeating because they reflect to a considerable extent the times in which they were produced. To achieve a cutout of this type, great skill was needed and a pair of exceedingly sharp scissors. The paper was folded first, sometimes several times, depending on the size and shape of the finished piece. Some were all white; some were cut from colored paper; while others were painted in vivid colors.

Now let us see what this young man had to say to his lady-fair. The lines are penned across the spread of the birds' wings, and at the center folds. By continually twisting and turning the valentine about, it is possible to make out the following:

1　February the fourteenth day
2　It's valentine they say
3　I choose you from among the rest
4　The reason was I loved you best
5　Sure as the grape grows on the vine
6　So sure you are my valentine
7　The rose is red the violet blue
8　Lilies are fair and so are you.

The ring in the center must be intended for number 9, though it is not so marked. It reads: "Round is the ring that has no end, so is my love for you my friend." The last four lines are written across the center folds, and wind up thus:

10　Again take this in good part
11　Along with it you have my heart

16

Plate 10. Handmade cutout valentine, c. 1790.

12 But if you do the same refuse
13 Pray burn this paper and me excuse.

The marked similarity of the verses and sentiment of this era are plainly noticeable. So are the symbols, such as the mating birds, the hearts, together with the simplicity of the creation as a whole, as against those of the Pennsylvania-Germans, which we shall soon examine. This valentine and those following in plates 11 and 12 may be of New England ancestry. The cutwork in the valentine shown in plate 11 is not as elaborate as many of this type, but again the symbols are pairs of birds and hearts. The penmanship is not particularly fine—and neither is the spelling! There are not many lines so let us consider what this swain had to offer. There is a numeral 1, so it is possible to tell where to begin.

Plate 11. American cutout valentine.

18

1 "The 14 day of February, it was my lot fer to be merry . . Lots was cast and one i drew . . kind fortune is it must be you . .

2 I choose you out amongst the rest . . It was becaus I love you best . . This valentine to you I send . . To prove I am your worthy friend . . But if you this valentine refuse . . Then burn it up if you choose . . And when the flame begin to rise. Think on the one you do despise."

Plate 12.

Handmade cutout, silhouette valentine, dated 1845.

And so the same theme, with minor variations, runs through these quaint love tokens of long ago. The later the date on cutouts, the more crude the workmanship is apt to be. However, plate 12 reveals a most charming silhouette valentine, which is a rarity of its type. The gentleman and his lady, the two cherubs, two pierced hearts, and the cupid with his trumpet, all combine into a most interesting composition. Its date is 1845.

A finer piece of cutwork than that displayed in plate 13 is rarely encountered. It is of considerable interest to have its history, too, for so often this has been lost by succeeding generations. This valentine was cut by Anne Seddon of Fredericksburg, Virginia, sometime prior to 1817. She married William H. Roy of Matthews County, Virginia. It is now owned by their granddaughter, Mrs. Bradley S. Johnson of Richmond.

A distinct type of workmanship was achieved by the Pennsylvania-Germans. Among collectors examples of their Fractur[1] is keenly sought, as well as their cutouts and pin prick work. All these items carry interesting symbols and unusual coloring, so they represent a different kind of art in themselves. The great difficulty is that Pennsylvania-German valentines, birth certificates, marriage certificates, love tokens, religious and decorative pieces, are written in German script, and so one specializing in valentines again has to be certain that he is really buying a valentine, rather than a love token, or any one of the various items named. They are all apt to be decorated with birds, hearts, tulips, and angels, usually in brilliant shades of red, blue, green, and yellow (with the exception of the angels!).

A prime example of Pennsylvania German Fractur and decorative motifs may be seen in plate 14, from the collection in the Metropolitan Museum. It is thought to date around 1814. The cutwork of pots of flowers, together with the arrangement of the hearts and flowers, is perhaps as magnificent a specimen of this type of work as may be found anywhere. The coloring measures up to the finest in Pennsylvania-German tradition. That these valentines were more often than not proposals of marriage, and a form of love-making that relieved the shy suitor of saying what was in his heart by proxy, is revealed in the translation of this German Fractur. The message in the hearts reads as follows:

1 My dear child, I cannot hide my heart any longer.
2 I have you—if you like it—selected as my beloved.
3 I will give you my heart if you want it.
4 In my thoughts I have kissed you often because you are such a pretty girl.
5 You are more to me in this world than wealth, fortune and money.
6 Will you now love me always and nobody else?
7 Then my heart is yours and I will love you until death.
8 Love is built only on faith.
9 Faith is the basis for love, faithlessness makes love disappear soon.

[1] A highly ornamental style of writing with fractures and much ornamentation. An adaptation of the Gothic type, usually employing primary or secondary colors. Term is taken from the Latin *fractura*, meaning break, fracture, or cleft but when applied to writing assumes a special meaning.

Plate 13.

Handcut valentine made before 1817.

10 If you will be faithful to me, only death will us part.
11 My heart always thinks of you, only faith do I enjoy.
12 My only wish is to make you happy and to be united with
      you in marriage.
13 I love you with all my heart, my dearest treasure.
14 My heart is all yours and I think of you at all hours.
15 Sweet treasure, if you will be faithful to me, I will be to you.
16 Faith is the duty of lovers, dearest treasure, don't forget it.

With this final admonition on the subject of faithfulness, his proposal of
marriage is concluded.

A rarity today which ardent collectors of valentines avidly seek, is a

Plate 14.

Pennsylvania-German cutout, with verse in
Fractur. c. 1814.

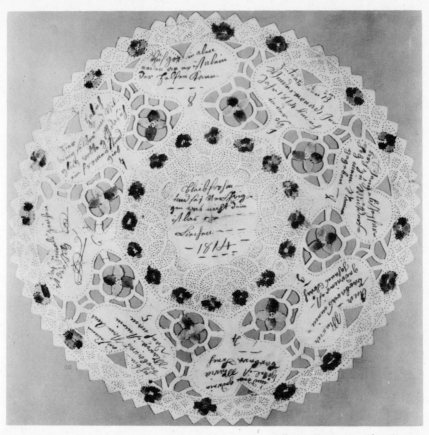

Plate 15.

Pennsylvania-German cutout and pinprick
work, dated 1814.

good example of Pennsylvania-German pinprick work. The valentine in
plate 15 is actually a museum piece, for the pinprick is combined with
cutwork, and the flowers interspersed throughout the charming design
are hand colored. The eight numbered hearts each contain lines in German script and, fortunately, the center is dated 1814, which establishes
the time. To create such a valentine one needed a penknife, very sharp
scissors, a needle and pin, plus artistic ability and a steady hand! One
can scarcely imagine the youth of today attempting to copy this work of
art—it would require too much time, and patience. The love of creating
by hand largely disappeared by 1850, though one occasionally sees some
cutwork of a slightly later date. Plate 16 contrasts sharply with the valentine just described. While it has charm, the style is more reminiscent

23

Norcross, New York

Plate 16.

Pennsylvania-German cutout, with some pinprick work, date 1854.

of great-grandmother's bed quilt design. The hearts in the border contain a small amount of pinprick work—eight of them prominently dated 1854. It would be difficult to be certain whether this valentine is of Pennsylvania origin or not, for it is a fallacy to believe all cutout and pinprick work emanated from that one section of our country. Other examples have been found from other states: New England, Virginia, Maryland, New York, New Jersey, and Ohio. Of course, wherever the Pennsylvania-Germans migrated from Pennsylvania in the early days, examples of their work were bound to be discovered, sooner or later.

Four examples of choice little heart-shaped love tokens, one dated 1829, and one or more of which may have been intended as a valentine, are illustrated in plate 17. These are all handmade cutouts, hand painted

24

Plate 17.

Norcross, New York

Handmade love tokens, one dated 1829.

with delicate leaves and flowers. Three are penned in English script, while the dated one is in Fractur. Such pieces are an interesting addition to any collection, as they are early and rare, whether or not they were intended as valentines.

Other types of handmade hearts are like those illustrated in plate 18. As may be noted, one is a single heart and the other is double. In one fell swoop a youth could offer his hand and heart! The woven design on the back of the hands, as well as through the center of one of the hearts, involved some intricate work. The double heart was handed down through several generations of a Connecticut family, where it was finally discovered between the leaves of a family Bible.

The Pennsylvania-German cutouts were not always elaborate nor were they necessarily hand painted in bright colors. Plate 19 displays a comparatively simple one, featuring the heart motif, with a small amount of pin prick work added. Such pieces are quaint and have a certain amount of decorative value.

That the vogue for handmade valentines spread far and wide in this country a century and a quarter ago is evidenced by the two illustrated in plates 20 and 21. By one of those strange and almost unbelievable quirks of fate, these were found many miles apart, though both were created in 1830 by two girls who undoubedly never heard of each other. The valentines are similar in size and design and both feature birds. Besides hearts, six-pointed stars and tulips, other popular Pennsylvania-Ger-

Plate 18. Handmade valentines.

Plate 19.

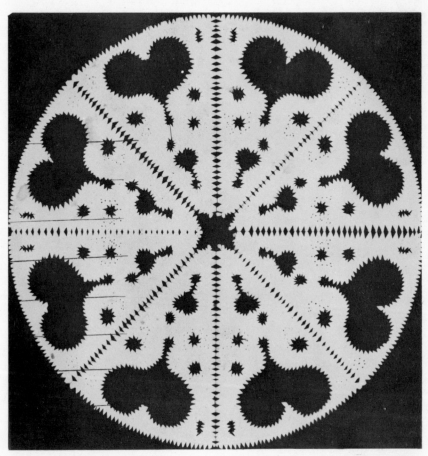

Pennsylvania-German cutout and pinprick,
featuring heart motif.

27

man motifs include the "distelfink bird,"[1] as well as doves. It may be noted that the birds above the main part of the design, as well as the branches below, bear a striking resemblance. The valentine in plate 20 was signed Miss Sarah Gracey, "June 20th in the year of our Lord one thousand eight hundred and thirty." It was a belated message and, despite the date must be included among valentines because of the wording. It starts off thus:

> "I hope you will not take amiss,
> My being so bold as to send you this.
> Lots were cast and One I drew,
> My fortune was to meet with you,
> I chose you from among the rest
> The reason was I loved you best
> Sure as the grapes grew on the vine
> I choose you for my valentine
> The rose is red, the grape is green
> The days are past that I have seen—
> The roses red, the violet blue,
> Carnations are sweet and so are you
> If you love me as I love you
> No knife shall cut our love in two
> Search all the valleys, hills and planes
> And shady groves where Cupid reigns
> For you to find out my Bleeding Heart
> That I may escape its venoms dart,
> And if by chance you find it there
> Conduct it home to me with care
> For your reward so well shall be
> With such like kind fidelity."

The balance of the verses run on in like vein. It is unusual to find valentines written by girls, and this is one reason why the two are illustrated and quoted here.

Plate 21 is an *answer* sent by a young lady to her suitor. Note, if you will, the direct approach!

> "Dear Sir: Indeed your very kind,
> I'm quite overjoy'd to know your mind,
> I did receive your valentine,
> Now in return I send you mine.

[1] European finch.

28

Plate 20.

Pennsylvania-German cutout valentine, hand
colored, dated 1830.

Plate 21.

Pennsylvania-German cutout, hand colored,
dated 1830.

30

Mariah Owen

May art and nature both combine
And make thy native beauties shine
Robe them in innocence so fair
Implant the seeds of virtue there
And when thy years to ripeness come
Have fame and virtue all thy own
On evry tongue thy name shall sound
With sentiments the most sublime
O'er when dull time has run its round
No one shall say but Glory's thine

Norcross, New York

Plate 22.

Pennsylvania-German pen-and-ink valentine,
to Mariah Owen.

Now if your words express your mind,
A heart as true in me you'll find,
I'll keep it safe, I'll love the name,
I'll place it in a golden frame
I've been weak enough to let you know
As this my valentine doth show
Hope to a lover's mind is sweet
Therefore I hope we soon will meet
Farewell, therefore, til next we meet
Tis heaven on earth my love to greet
Hymen will bless when Cupid's dart
Has pierced two lovers to the heart."

And so the young man is accepted, and the path now lies open for him to appear with "Round is the ring that has no end."

Plate 22 illustrates a rather unusual bit of Pennsylvania-German workmanship in pen and ink. It was done with brown ink on a light brown paper, the poem being dedicated to Mariah Owen. It is a graceful design, dating about 1820.

Another different type of handmade valentine made its appearance quite early, though it would be hazardous to state exactly how early. This particular style is known as Theorem work, or Poonah, an Oriental style of painting. It was achieved by drawing or tracing each element of the design on oil paper. From this a stencil was cut and water colors were utilized through the perforations; then mixed gum arabic was applied with a stiff brush, which fixed the pattern. The same method, which was really a type of stencil work, was sometimes used in making the quaint old paintings on velvet. Plates 23 and 24 show two valentines produced by the Theorem method. The first, with red flowers and green leaves, is thought to date about 1835-1840. The one in plate 24 was made by Amanda Snowball, and is dated "Manchester, Feby 1849." The creases in the paper are due to the fact that it was folded and posted by hand. The design is a snowball, on which a red bird with blue wings rests on a tree branch. In dainty Spencerian handwriting are penned the following lines:

"I've often thought that I would send,
A valentine to some dear friend,
Now, though I've many friends, 'tis true,
My preference is all for you,
For if the truth must be confess'd,
Believe me, I like you the best."

This valentine was made on a double sheet of pale blue-gray paper.

Plate 23.

American Theorem work, 1835–1840.

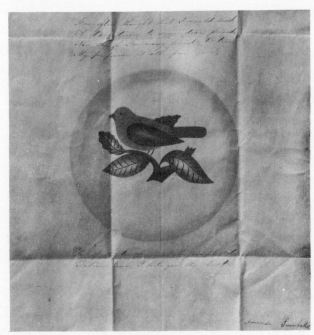

Plate 24.

Theorem work by Amanda Snowball, dated 1849.

(See also color supplement between pages 106 and 107.)

33

Theorem work was popular among girls at boarding schools, during the 1840's.

A quaint form of handmade valentine difficult to find today is one which features an old-time tintype, picturing either the maid or the youth as shown in plate 25. This kind of valentine was often made on embossed or decorated letter paper, and then further embellished by hand. The vines were painted and the flowers pasted on. It dates about 1840.

Another daguerreotype valentine, which dates around 1842, is shown in plate 26. The embossed border has been hand painted, and the envelope was homemade. A main point of interest is the name "Donaldson —New York," across the lower border. Pasqual Donaldson was a producer of valentines in New York between 1839 and 1855. He was listed at various addresses, including 178 Orchard Street.

Valentines of a simpler nature, written on decorated letter paper, may be encountered from time to time. An attractive one is shown in plate 27, with a hand-painted rose in the upper corner. This was directed "To Hetty." An appropriate verse followed, and it is signed "St. Valentine's Morn 1846." Special embossed letter sheets were sold for valentine verses as early as 1783.

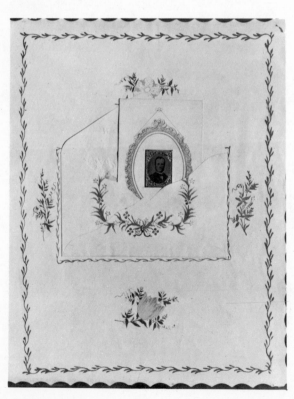

Norcross, New York

Plate 25.

Letter-paper valentine, with daguerreotype, c. 1840.

Plate 26.

Letter-paper valentine by P. Donaldson, New York, c. 1842.

Plate 27.

Letter-paper valentine, dated 1846.

35

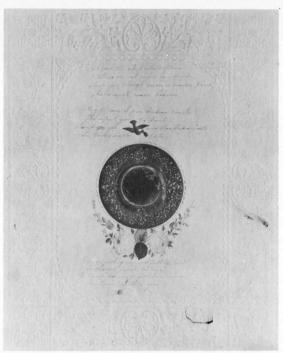

Plate 28.

Mirror valentine by T. W. Strong, New York,
c. 1845.

T. W. Strong's lithographs may be encountered much more frequently today than his handmade valentines, such as the one illustrated in plate 28. The paper with the embossed border antedates the perforated lace edge. While the particular paper on which this valentine was created bears an embossed "Strong, N. Y." it must have been made up on order for him in England, as it is a pattern known to have been produced by Mansell. This valentine dates from about 1845, during which period embossed papers of this type were not being made here. The verse is the homemade variety, the flowers pasted on and the leaves in the background painted in by hand, as is typical of the 1845-1855 era. The mirror in the center is also a familiar form of adornment at this time.

Though it was not made in this country, it seems appropriate to illustrate here one of the three oldest known valentines in America (plate 29). Probably originally emanating from Strasbourg it is an exquisite bit of handwork, lettered in German "I ever will in you remain, So let your heart return again." Said to be circa 1710, much of this type of work is claimed to have been accomplished by nuns in Germany for the

Plate 29.

One of the oldest
known valentines in
America, thought to
have been made by
nuns in Strasbourg,
c. 1710.

Norcross, **New York**

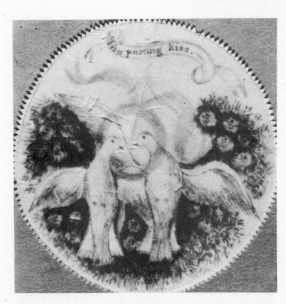

Plate 30.

Hand-painted valen-
tine, watchpaper.

Norcross, New York

37

benefit of charity. The sender undoubtedly added his message to the completed valentine.

Another branch of collecting are watchpapers. They were produced by practically every method known to valentines, and thus may be found in prick; engraved and hand colored; lithographed; in paper lace, etc. These water color, such as the one pictured in plate 30; or in cutout and pin-prick; engraved and hand colored; lithographed; in paper lace, etc. These little watchpapers were popular in the days when men carried pocket watches, and they were made in a size to fit within the back or front cover of the watch. In size they measure from two inches in diameter to two-and-a-half inches. The one illustrated here shows two fluttering doves, their heads within a wedding ring, and a shadowy dart points to a ribbon, inscribed, "The parting kiss." These dainty bits of handwork are particularly difficult to find today, though a number of collectors have specialized in them. Because some have turned up that were obviously valentine gifts, they are included in this chapter.

III

AMERICAN LITHOGRAPHED VALENTINES

1840 — 1860

PRIOR TO THE tidal wave created by the great popularity of the lace-edged sentimental valentines, which surged over this country around 1850, lithographs and woodcuts made their appearance. We were in the midst of a great transitional era between 1840 and 1850, when craftsmanship in many lines was undergoing rapid changes. It was the beginning of the great machine age—which historians call the Industrial Revolution. While the ladies fair still received handmade valentines, they now also become recipients of newer styles effected by various processes. While some were engraved or made from woodcuts, by and large they were mostly lithographs and hand colored. These were the forerunners of the embossed or lace-bordered valentines. Imports along this line were few and far between prior to 1850. Moreover, we did not have any great artists here during this period, contemporaneous with the famous names in England.

An example of a delicate bit of designing may be seen in the lithographed valentine in plate 31, which was hand colored. This is dated February 14, 1840 and penned across it is:

> "May friendship's constant kiss be thine
> From this sweet day of valentine."

At this point, the printed valentines were often left open for the sender to write his message. The personal touch added a charm that was soon to be lost in the stereotyped verses which were turned out in enormous quantities. Turner & Fisher of Philadelphia published this valentine. The firm name is associated with Philadelphia, though Abraham Fisher was in business in New York early in the 1830's. He was born in 1812. How he happened to become associated with Frederick Turner is not known at present, but they were in business in Philadelphia from 1835, when they were listed as booksellers and publishers at 11 North Sixth Street, until 1849. In 1841 they moved to 15 North Sixth Street. Apparently their partnership terminated in 1849, because in 1850 Frederick Turner was in the stationery business alone.

Abraham Fisher first appears in New York directories in 1836, as hav-

Plate 31.　Hand-colored lithographed valentine by Turner
& Fisher of Philadelphia, dated 1840.

ing a book store at 90 Division Street. From 1839 until 1845, he was located at 52 Chatham Street, when he changed to 74 Chatham Street. He
lived at the same addresses as his stores until 1850, when he decided to
make his home in Philadelphia, though he still retained his book store
at 74 Chatham Street, with branches in Boston and Baltimore. A brother
was associated with him part of the time when they were known as Fisher
& Brother. Over the years, they turned out a great variety of valentines,
including comics, two of which may be seen in chapter VI. A German
comic by Fisher is in the collection of the New York Historical Society.
Fisher published many political cartoons prior to the Civil War.

　　Another early New York publisher was Elton & Company, of 18
Division Street. Robert Elton was producing valentines in 1833, and possibly earlier. Two examples of his work are shown in plate 32. While

he created various types, including comics, the two illustrated which were made expressly for children are typical of the times.

Perhaps one of the most prolific publishers of valentines in New York was T. W. Strong, as evidenced by the crowd admiring his store window at 98 Nassau Street (plate 33). Starting about 1842 at 153 Fulton Street, he built up an enormous business, one of his specialties being valentines of all sorts. As his advertisement in 1848 states: "Valentines! Valentines! All varieties of Valentines, imported and domestic, sentimental, humorous, witty, comic, serious, local, and national, got up in the most superb style on lace paper and gold, without regard to expense. Also, envelopes and Valentine Writers, and everything connected with Valentines, to suit all customers—prices varying from six cents to ten dollars; for sale wholesale and retail at Thomas W. Strong's Great Depot of Valentines, 98 Nassau Street." He published Valentine Writers, one being titled "People's Valentine Writer. By a Literary Lady." This is illustrated in plate 47. Many of the verses were addressed to various people or trades, such as "Harriet to her admirer" or "Frances to her Beau" or "To a Gentleman in the Navy." These little "verse writers" must have been in great demand, even though they were more or less looked down upon by the

Plate 32. Two lithographed valentines by Elton & Company, of New York.

American Antiquarian Society

Plate 33. T. W. Strong's Valentine Depot in New York, c. 1848.

literati as being too stereotyped. Their advent greatly hastened the commercialization of valentines, both here and in England.

Two typical Strong lithographed valentines may be seen in plates 34 and 35. Strong's usual identification marks are either "Strong, N. Y." or "T. W. Strong, 98 Nassau St. N. Y." or simply "98 Nassau St." The coloring of the lithographs is applied by hand, rather crudely. In the smaller valentine, the lady's dress is pale blue; she is wearing a deep rose-red coat, and the bench is draped in yellow which conveniently matches the gentleman's trousers, which are a yellow check. His coat is a deep blue-black. One end of the bench is pink, as well as the flower urn behind them. The trees are partly blue-green and yellow-green, the light coloring possibly to suggest late spring. For the time being, the fact that St. Valentine's Day falls on February 14 is forgotten by the ardent lovers! The larger valentine in plate 35 has less color. The maiden's gown is deep rose-red, and the gentleman is wearing a brown coat, blue waistcoat, and white trousers. The roses in the background are red. The familiar symbols of St. Valentine's Day are not so prominent during this particular period, though they are beginning to be noted, such as cupids, hearts, and the inevitable church with the waiting coach, suggest-

42

ing a wedding. Later on, mating birds, lambs, pierced hearts, and wedding rings figure more prominently in the decoration. A handmade valentine by Strong, with an embossed edge, is illustrated and described in chapter II.

Popular for a time along about 1850 were engraved valentines in the form of bank notes, such as the one issued in 1850, pictured in plate 36. This one was drawn on "the Bank of True Love, secured by the Pledge of the whole stock of Truth, Honor, and Fidelity, in the State of Matrimony." The bearer states "I promise to pay to . . . . on acceptance the sincere homage and never failing devotion of an affectionate heart. Hymen, Cash^r, Cupid, Pres^t." This attractively decorated item is inscribed, "Lith. D. Haring, 83 Canal St." and in the lower left-hand corner: "Richard Marsh, 374 Pearl St., New York. Valentine's Depot."

Author's Collection

Plate 34.   Early hand-colored lithograph by T. W. Strong, New York, and another on embossed paper, maker unknown.

The "Bank of Love" notes were issued in England also, but their popularity was short-lived, since they were considered to be too dangerously like the real thing. They were not only banned—they were recalled! It is quite possible the same fate may have befallen them here as all such valentines in the form of bank notes are fairly rare today.

Plate 37 discloses a particularly choice lithographed valentine by Keffer & Brett of Philadelphia. No such firm name appears in the city direc-

I felt warm friendship first for thee,
My beauteous Valentine,
And thought how happy I could be,
Were thy true friendship mine!

But, sweet one, on a second thought,
My bosom sighs for more,
Though rich the joys thy friendship brought,
Love hath a richer store.

T. W. Strong, 98 Nassau st., N. Y

Plate 35.

Hand-colored lithograph by T. W. Strong,
New York.

tories, though John Keffer was named as a lithographer at 12 Bank Street, in 1847. The American Antiquarian Society in Worcester, Massachusetts, has a J. L. Keffer lithograph of 1856, and Harry Peters notes a J. L. Keffer as a lithographer in Philadelphia in 1839. Apparently his name is not generally associated with valentines, and any examples by him must be considered rare.

An extremely rare hand-colored lithograph by an almost unknown lithographer is displayed in plate 38. Beneath the wreath of flowers is printed, "Drawn on stone by D. W. Moody," and near the lower border it is further inscribed, "Lith. of W. Moody, 140 Nassau St. N. York." Considerable hand work is involved in this valentine, for there is more to it than meets the eye at a casual glance. The lithograph was completed, colored, and then the design on the inner portion of the large wreath was laboriously cut out, carefully following the line of each flower and leaf. The smaller wreath was entirely removed and the outer edge trimmed around the flowers. The valentine was then mounted on white satin, the smaller wreath being attached to the center. In terms of present-day labor costs, this would be an expensive valentine to produce. However, it is entirely possible that it was purchased by a love-lorn youth or damsel, who inserted the satin center in an effort to create a more ornate effect. What is important is that Moody's lithograph on stone is rare. He was listed in a New York directory of 1846 as David W. Moody, lithographer, and in 1849 as a "draughtsman" of 128 Fulton Street. No other mention of him could be found.

Many valentines were published during the Civil War, for the benefit of soldiers and civilians alike. One which is eagerly sought by collectors

Plate 36.

Engraved valentine bank note lithographed by
D. Haring, 83 Canal Street, New York. *Author's Collection*

45

Plate 37.

Early lithograph by Keffer & Brett of Philadelphia.

Plate 38.

Rare hand-colored lithograph by D. W. Moody, of New York.

is reproduced in plate 39, the first view showing the tent flaps open, and the second closed. Plate 40 illustrates the attractive envelopes in which the valentines were sent, one being elaborately lithographed and the other embossed. The top example was mailed to Miss Cordelia Guids of Mapleville, Rhode Island, and the embossed envelope to Miss Ella Clemence of Worcester, Massachusetts, from Old Point Comfort, Virginia, on February 26, 1863. Many firms advertised valentines for soldiers at this period, though it is difficult to find these Civil War items today.

While there were other producers of lithographed valentines in the United States and literally thousands of examples could be shown, they are all similar in style. These particular illustrations are therefore being limited in number so that more space may be devoted to the wider variety of other types. Most of the American lithographers are represented in the chapter on comics.

Boston can lay claim to one publisher of greeting cards, who became well known during the 1870's and 1880's, although not primarily because of valentines. His name was Louis Prang. Prang was born in Breslau, Prussian Silesia, on May 12, 1824. He acquired a training in the technique of dyeing and printing calico in his father's factory, though he studied with other firms in several countries of Europe, before coming to the United States.

Louis Prang landed in New York on April 5, 1850. He went on to Boston, where his beginnings in the business world, first as a publisher and then in the leather business, proved of short duration. His next venture was in wood engraving. For a time he worked under Frank Leslie, then head of the art department of *Gleason's Pictorial*. In 1856 he started in business as a lithographer in partnership with Julius Mayer, and operated under the name of Prang & Mayer. However, along about 1860 this partnership was dissolved, and he began for himself as L. Prang & Company. Both energetic and enterprising, he soon found himself making money. It has been said that he was constantly devising novelties. During the Civil War he published and sold large numbers of maps, showing the territory where battles were being fought. A trip to Europe in 1864 resulted in his becoming interested in the reproduction of famous works of art, by way of colored lithography. The *Printing Times* of London stated on January 15, 1875 that "Mr. Prang was the first to apply . . . the designation of 'chromos' to this type of colored lithograph."

In 1867 Louis Prang established a printing establishment in Roxbury, Massachusetts, where he not only reproduced chromos, but went into various other lines, including Christmas cards. These he first sold in England where they were contemporaneous with Marcus Ward's greeting cards, together with those of Raphael Tuck & Sons, as well as other competitors. In 1875 he introduced Christmas cards to the American market.

47

These were either plain or edged with silk fringe, and were characterized by their delicate coloring. They were not symbolical of the season, but employed flowers, kittens, skating scenes, etc.

Out of sixty-seven volumes devoted to Prang's greeting cards in the American Antiquarian Society at Worcester, Massachusetts, exactly one thin book contained valentines. Apparently Louis Prang had little regard

Plate 39. Two views of a Civil War valentine.

for the patron saint of lovers! However, this may indicate that his valentine cards are a scarce item today. A collector would be justified in not feeling too regretful, judging by the samples before me now. One page contains four cards the size of modern place cards, done in pastel colors. Each carries a bust of a little girl, lettered "Thine, ever thine," or "St. Valentine greets you." Four samples on another page are even smaller, each having a spray of pansies, wild roses, or morning glories. Others carry a single pansy, marked, "My valentine, Think of me." Still other pages have heart-shaped frames containing exactly the same little girl's face as on the first page. The single hearts finally develop into interlocking double hearts of flowers, with messages in the center. Finally twelve cards in a larger size (5 by 4 inches) emerge, all bearing naked cupids engaged

Plate 40.

Two Civil War valentine envelopes.

in various occupations, such as peering out of a window, picking flowers, nesting in a rose bush, or crawling into a basket as shown in plate 195. This last one is marked "Copyright 1893, L. Prang & Co., Boston." The cards sold for sixty cents per dozen.

One novelty, illustrated in plate 196, reproduces the form of a large red tomato, which is marked in embossed gold lettering, "Love Apple." Years ago tomatoes were sometimes planted in flower gardens and were actually referred to as "love apples." They were not considered edible in those days, as many believed they would cause cancer. Thus the tomato was utilized as a design for an ornamental valentine, and sold in individual boxes at $7.20 per dozen.

A Prang sample book contained one unusual design (plate 197) which is reminiscent of Walter Crane and Kate Greenaway. Actually it is the only specimen displaying character and fine, deep coloring. It was copyrighted in 1882. A collector could add these particular Prang valentine cards to his collection without misgivings.

IV

ESTHER HOWLAND'S VALENTINES

A BOOK ON VALENTINES would not be complete without telling the story of Esther Howland. Special recognition must be accorded this lady for her unique accomplishments—she built up a business which eventually ran into sales of $100,000 annually: this in the days when a career woman was a *rara avis*. Indeed, woman's place was traditionally in the home, and it was neither fashionable nor popular to have any connection with the business world—before two world wars forced many changes upon us.

Esther Allen Howland was the only daughter of Southworth A. and Esther Howland of 16 Summer Street, Worcester, Massachusetts. She was born August 17, 1828 and graduated from Mount Holyoke College in 1847. Not very many women were university graduates then! Miss How-land's father was the leading stationer and bookseller of Worcester, the firm name being S. A. Howland & Sons. Besides Esther, there were three younger brothers, Charles Allen, Edward Payson, and William Otis. They were the seventh generation of direct descent of John Howland, one of the Pilgrim fathers.

So many, many stories have been written about Esther Howland over the intervening years since her death nearly half a century ago that it has become difficult to separate the chaff from the wheat. For instance, Miss Bertha E. Blakely, Librarian Emeritus of Mount Holyoke College wrote: "Miss Howland was graduate of the year 1847 and died in 1904. The in-formation we have has come from newspaper clippings. We think that most of the clippings which come year by year have been prepared from earlier clippings. We have no more source material than this." Despite this discouraging news it has been possible, after checking and rechecking, to piece together something of the story of this remarkable girl. However, before closing the subject of her being a Mount Holyoke graduate, it was ironic to learn that Emily Dickinson, who also attended there, wrote to her brother, Austin Dickinson, under date of February 14, 1848, saying: "Monday afternoon Mistress Lyon arose in the hall and forbade our send-ing any of those foolish notes called valentines." It may be wondered if

"Mistress Lyon" lived to hear of the fortune Esther Howland amassed as a result of "those foolish notes"!

The same year Esther graduated from college, she received her first English valentine. It has been described as having an elaborate border of fine lace paper, and was decorated with colored flowers which had been cut out and pasted on. In the center was a small envelope faced with green paper, within which was placed a red-edged note containing the fervent sentiments appropriate to St. Valentine's Day. The description of this first English valentine sent Miss Howland is in keeping with the period when they were being made in Great Britain. She was so excited and pleased with it that she showed it to all her friends, who found it equally charming. Her father was impressed by the enthusiastic response the valentine elicited to the point that he concluded to import a few. When the shipment arrived, Esther was completely fascinated by them, and was impelled to try her hand at making one. It is claimed that she cut up some of the embossed valentine envelopes and, with the aid of some colored pictures, pasted them on a plain piece of paper, thus evolving her first valentine. After that, one followed another.

Esther's father must have recognized her artistic ability from her first samples, because he was easily persuaded to order materials for her from England in the way of lace paper, paper flowers, and colored paper, which were unobtainable in this country. When these arrived, she made up two particularly fine examples. They turned out so well that she soon had a dozen or more designs. Her brother Allen, who traveled for the Howland concern, was about to leave on one of his selling trips, and Esther asked him to take along her samples and see if he could dispose of a few. He traveled by horse and buggy each fall through northern Massachusetts, Vermont, and New Hampshire. She estimated he might possibly take orders for one or two hundred dollars' worth. When he returned with orders amounting to five thousand dollars in value, she was stunned. This sum represented enough work to keep her busy for several years!

Such an enormous undertaking might well have dismayed most people but not an ambitious, energetic person like Miss Howland. Her family gathered together, the matter was thoroughly discussed and a plan of action was decided upon. Embossed and perforated lace paper blanks and embossed envelopes were ordered from England and Mr. Howland went to New York and purchased colored pictures and other trimming from George Snyder, said to be the only lithographer having such materials for sale in this country at the time.

All the ingredients on hand, Esther asked several of her friends for assistance. A big room was set aside in the large Howland residence on Summer Street, where the work of completing the valentine orders was begun. Esther cut the basic designs for the cards the girls were to copy.

WHERE THE FIRST FANCY VALENTINE WAS MADE
IN THIS COUNTRY

Plate 41.

Esther Howland as she appeared in her fifties, and her home where the valentines were made. *Center*, one of her earliest creations, produced on Mansell lace paper.

53

Plate 42.

An "assembly line" of girls making valentines
during the 1850's.

Each girl was assigned a special task. One cut out pictures and kept them assorted in boxes. Another, with models to work from, made the backgrounds, passing them to still another who gave them further embellishment. So the sentimental valentines went on and on, from hand to hand, until finally the last one called for in the orders had been completed.

By the end of 1849 Esther Howland was firmly launched in the valentine business and technique. Instead of crediting Henry Ford with "mass production" innovations, it appears the honor should go to Miss Howland as the first with progressive assembly. This girl in her early twenties was possessed of a rare combination of qualities—artistic ability, business acumen, organization, plenty of good sense, plus unbounded energy. Here were all the ingredients required for a success story!

The first advertisement of Esther's valentines appeared in the Worcester, Massachusetts, *Daily Spy* under the date of February 5, 1850 and read: "Valentines. Persons wishing to select from the best assortment in the City are invited to call on S. A. Howland, 143 Main Street." This advertisement ran for two weeks.

The following year Miss Howland looked about for novelties, so that when her brother was ready to leave on his next selling trip, he was provided with a larger assortment than previously. Many of these were elaborate and expensive, among them being the first one she attempted carry-

Plate 43.

Two of Esther Howland's valentines, decorated with colored wafers of paper under the lace.

Plate 44.

Four of Esther Howland's
valentines of the early 1850's.

Author's Collection

56

ing a message from Cupid, in which silk or satin was utilized. One of her girls painted the silk centers with flowers, etc., which eventually brought about a tragedy. The artist had formed the habit of moistening the brush with her lips and in this way she finally absorbed so much of the paint that she died from the effects. Thereupon the valentines having painted silk or satin centers were discontinued.

When Miss Howland's brother returned from his selling expedition, the valentine orders were doubled. The working force was increased accordingly and now the third floor under the mansard roof was given over to the valentine factory. A long table was installed to facilitate the passing of the valentines. A skylight provided plenty of sunshine in summer, while the girls worked by gas light during the hours of dusk in winter.

Along about this time Esther conceived the idea of making dies, which she knew would do away with much laborious and tiresome cutting with scissors, a time-consuming task. She communicated with the German firm with whom she did business with reference to having cutting and embossing dies made so they could do the work for her. This the Germans declined to do—they were much too cagey for that even in the 1850's! They had their own dies made at less cost over there. Within a comparatively short time, embossed and cut pictures were on the market but the only remuneration Esther Howland received for her idea was the privilege of buying her paper valentine trimming in more convenient form.

Valentine's were not Esther Howland's sole interest. There followed Christmas and New Year's cards, birthday cards, booklets of various sorts —and May baskets! Esther was fond of telling a story about her most elaborate May basket and its disastrous consequences. As May Day approached, she concluded she would make up one sample May basket that would be the most gorgeous creation she could possibly conceive. When it was completed, it was placed on display for all to admire, and priced at ten dollars. Along came an enamored youth who could not resist it. He anticipated that the heart and hand of his lady-fair would surely be his when she beheld this beautiful basket and realized what she must mean to him to be given such an obviously expensive gift. But alack and alas! When the young lady inadvertently heard what it cost, she said she would have nothing more to do with such a wastrel. A young man who would throw his money away in such a manner would never make a suitable husband! So, a thrifty nature triumphed over love! When the sad tale reached Miss Howland's ears, she said there would be no more ten-dollar May baskets—at least not for New England trade!

As the years passed, the valentine business of Esther Howland flourished. Cards were sent all over the country. Deliveries in Worcester were made from a one-horse, two-wheeled shay. The volume swelled to $75,000 annually, then to $100,000. When business was at its height, an accident befell Esther. In Boston on a business trip, she fell on an icy sidewalk and injured her kneecap badly. In fact, it was so seriously hurt that for several years she superintended her business from a wheelchair. It may have been during this period that a New York concern who was purchasing $25,000 of her valentines annually made a liberal offer to control her output. Failing in this, they tried to buy her out altogether and were again refused.

As for Esther Howland's valentines, it may be said that they were always in good taste. She purchased the finest embossed and perforated blanks from such well-known English makers as Mansell, Wood, Mullord, Windsor, etc. "Blanks" were embossed or lace-edged folders, which could be decorated by hand. Just as certain glass manufacturers have made "blanks"—perfectly plain objects which are sold to other concerns who do the cutting or other ornamentation—valentine manufacturers prepared their own designs on ornamented paper specially created for that purpose. For instance, the center of such a sheet could be cut out and satin or silk inserted. This center would then be painted, or a built-up basket or vase of flowers would be placed against it, or perhaps a mirror attached to capture the face of the pretty recipient. Early valentines had little flowers carefully glued on, and the leaves or vines were often painted in by hand, as surrounding for the center attraction. Later on German-made heavily embossed, brightly colored "swags" or "scrap" of flowers, birds, or children replaced the more delicate flowers and handwork. Swags were sold in sheets, and examples of some of these, still in sheets, which never saw service, are shown in plate 177. A full-sized sheet measured 5½ by 9½ inches.

For several years after Esther Howland built and expanded her valentine business, she is reputed to have been alone in the field of the sentimental lace-type valentine. Whatever else, she certainly gained a corner on this market, selling vast quantities to New York dealers. Undoubtedly because of this it has often been claimed in recent articles on the subject, that she actually made the first valentines in our country. This statement is not quite true. Handmade valentines were known here for more than half a century, and other types were being produced, chiefly by New York manufacturers, for a number of years before she started in business. She may very well have been the first to create the English type of hand-decorated valentine in quantity, commercially. Thus she had little competition, except for imports, which were very expensive.

So the days lengthened into years for the merry little family of Howland valentine makers. It could not have seemed much like work to put together the fascinating bits of lace paper and decorative trimmings. It has been claimed that swains thought nothing of paying five or ten dollars for some of the Howland creations, many of which were sold from the stationery store of S. A. Howland & Sons.

Plate 45.

A Howland valentine in gold and yellow, of
the early 1860's.

Esther Howland is credited with several innovations; however, all these are not easily verified. She is said to have been the first to use small, brightly colored glazed wafers of paper, usually about an inch in diameter, which she placed effectively in corners, or other appropriate spots, under the lace paper. By this colorful device the whiteness of the valentine was relieved. Many Howland designs are spotted in New England by these discs of vivid green, yellow, red, and other shades. This particular type of valentine would appear to date in the late 1850's and early 1860's, although she never entirely abandoned the use of the brightly hued wafers.

Esther had an aversion to mottoes on the outside of her valentines. Instead, she used conventional verses, printed and lithographed on small slips, which were pasted on the inside page. They undoubtedly came in sheets and were cut apart and inserted by her girls. These printed verses, too, are said to have been her original idea.

Introduction of the "lift-up" valentine must also be credited to Miss Howland. This innovation consisted of several paper-lace motifs, which were built up in tiers so that when one looked through the openings a pleasant perspective was thereby provided for the picture in the center. This type was particularly effective when placed in an ornamental box, made for the purpose. Another simpler method of building up the cards, again believed to have been a product of her fertile brain, was attained by the use of two or more narrow pieces of heavy paper, folded three times. These little folders, first attached to the body of the valentine and then to another layer of lace, lifted the lace above the foundation so that it not only stood out but stayed in place. Esther Howland, in other words, was responsible for a basic change in valentine styles. They remained built-up affairs, gradually growing more and more elaborate with the passing of the years—until they literally collapsed from their own weight. However, during her time they were never massive. It is to her credit that she accomplished the switch-over from handmade valentines to those which were merely put together by hand. After all, we had reached a progressive period in our nation's history, and she was a progressive young woman.

An identifying mark for Howland valentines is a small letter "H" stamped in red, on either an upper or lower corner of the back page. A few have been found with a tiny white heart glued on the back, having a red "H" in the center. A third manner of marking was a small label, printed with a red "H," this label also being glued on. Most of these marks are accompanied by numerals, which probably indicated size. Since Miss Howland purchased her valentine papers from England, it is not at all unusual to find a valentine embossed with the name of Wood, Mullord, or Windsor on the face and the tell-tale little red "H" on the back.

Plate 46.

Two Howland pull-out valentines of the late
1860's.

Her only other mark was the embossed "N.E.V.Co.," which we shall explain presently.

At least during her earlier years in the business Miss Howland inspected every valentine that went out. She was a strict business woman, but seems to have held the affection of her girls. It has been claimed that she reorganized her business in 1860, and this may very well be true, for the volume had grown so large that some changes in methods of making and distributing the cards must have been in order. She went to New York alone on a business trip about this time, which occasioned a certain amount of caustic comment. The fact that she was met there by an uncle did not lessen the criticism. Young ladies simply did not take business trips alone in those days! So someone is reported to have referred to her as a hussy! This is rather surprising for Worcester, which, as the late George Apley reminded us, is not Boston.

Esther Howland's father apparently took an active interest in her affairs, for a time, at least. He published *The Ladies and Gentlemen's Sentimental Valentine Writer*, which is illustrated in plate 47. These aids to the lovelorn contained verses designed to assist those who wrote their own valentines. However, with the rapid growth of Esther's valentine business, Mr. Howland evidently decided to leave his daughter a clear

Plate 47. Four Valentine Writers dating from May 1823
until the 1850's.

field, for he embarked in the insurance business, according to Worcester
city directories, in 1856. From that year until 1871 he is listed at eight
different business addresses in Worcester. Until 1876 one of his insurance
advertisements contained this notice, "Office of New England Valentine
Co."

At this time two other names connected with the valentine business
in Worcester appear, one or both of whom had some bearing on Esther
Howland's affairs. These two were Jotham W. Taft and his son, Edward.
Not too much is known about either one. Jotham Taft was born on February 3, 1816 and lived to attain the ripe old age of 94. Some of his youth
was spent in Connecticut, but from 1857 until 1862 he was a shoemaker
in Worcester. In 1863 he was listed with "valentines" after his name.
Apparently Jotham was an "in and outer" for he was also a "fancy perfumer," had to do with an "eating house," and in 1889 was a "valentine
manufacturer." Strange as it may seem, he wound up as an elevator op-
erator! That he did make some really pretty valentines may be attested
by some in my own collection, bearing an embossed "Taft" on the back
page. One of my boxed valentines, illustrated in plate 48, carries a Taft
label printed in red similar to those Esther Howland used. So at inter-

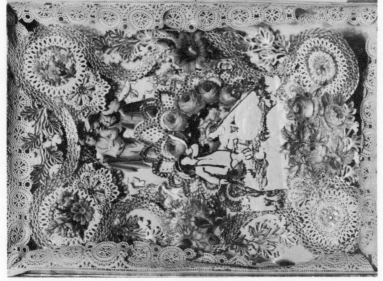

Plate 48. A boxed valentine bearing a Taft label.

vals during his career he did make attractive valentines. Other examples of his work exist in the large collection of the American Antiquarian Society. There have been vague reports to the effect that he worked for Esther Howland for a time and some have thought she sold out to him, when she retired. However, Jotham Taft had a son Edward, who appears in Worcester directories as a "valentine maker" from 1877 until 1880, and Edward undoubtedly became associated with Esther Howland.

Sometime after Miss Howland reorganized her business she apparently formed the "New England Valentine Co." Valentines are not too difficult to find locally, marked on the back page with an embossed "N.E.V.Co." In my own collection there are several so marked, all appearing to be of the 1870's. Four are shown in plate 49. One has the embossed "N.E.V.Co." covered by one of Esther's labels bearing her usual red "H." Since this company name does not appear in any Worcester directory until 1874, it seems likely that Miss Howland adopted it in the early seventies.

In 1879 Esther Howland published *The New England Valentine Co.'s Valentine Verse Book for 1879.* It contained thirty-one pages of verses printed in red, green, gold, and blue. There was a total of 131 verses made in three different sizes. Miss Howland stated: "This Book is designed for the trade selling our goods exclusively, and is furnished gratuitously. It meets the wants of those purchasing valentines to send to their friends. It is frequently the case that a valentine is found to suit, but the verse or sentiment is not right. In a case like this, the book is given them, and one is selected, cut out, and pasted over, making it satisfactory." This unique offering was "published by the New England Valentine Co., 425 Main Street, Worcester, Mass.," and speaks for itself.

Miss Howland continued to do business from her home until about 1879, when the New England Valentine Company moved to the new address at 425 Main Street and continued there through 1880. As Edward Taft's business address was also 425 Main Street during 1879 and 1880, he must have worked with or for, Esther Howland. That neither of their names are given for this address again, and since Edward in 1881 "removed to N. E. village," would appear to indicate that she sold out to the George C. Whitney Company before 1881. That she could not have had further business dealings with Edward's father, Jotham Taft, is certain because by 1889, when he re-engaged in the valentine business, Esther was no longer living in Worcester. There was a reason for this.

Shortly after Miss Howland's mother died, her father was in an accident that left him nearly helpless. Being a dutiful daughter, she decided her place was at his side and therefore she must give up her business to look after him. Her name appeared in the Worcester directory of 1880 sans a business address for the first time. However, her brother William

64

Plate 49.

Four Howland valentines marked "N.E.V. Co."

was interested in valentines in 1881, so it is quite possible he handled the disposal of her business, since she was busily engaged caring for her father at this time.

Esther Howland's father died on October 7, 1882, at the age of 82. She continued to stay on at the family home until 1886, when she moved to Quincy, Massachusetts, to live with her brother Charles, at 2 Adams Street. It was in Quincy where Esther Howland, a spinster all her life, died on March 15, 1904, at the age of 75 years, 6 months, and 24 days.

From the scissors and paste-pot of Esther Howland's girls to the giant machinery of the George C. Whitney Company represents a span of thirty years but the gulf is as deep and wide as was the sunny room at 16 Summer Street, where the Howland girls assembled their pretty sentimental valentines, to the 75,000 feet of floor space in the modern Whitney plant at 67 Union Street. The wheels of the machine age are vastly more rapid than girlish hands but the charm provided by the human touch has gone.

V

GEORGE C. WHITNEY & COMPANY

GEORGE C. WHITNEY followed in the wake of Esther Howland, though he was for a time contemporaneous with her. Indeed, a member of the family once asserted that had it not been for the nation-wide interest Miss Howland aroused in valentines, the well-known Whitney greeting card business might never have existed.

George C. Whitney was born in Westminster, Massachusetts, September 19, 1842. His schooling was interrupted by the Civil War, in which he fought with the Fifty-First Regiment of Massachusetts Volunteers. He was honorably discharged from the army when he was mustered out in 1863 and thereafter took a clerical position for a year or so.

While biographical sketches of the life of George Whitney have little to say of his brothers, records taken from the Worcester city directories indicate that the valentine business was originally very much of a family affair. George had two elder brothers, Sumner, born June 27, 1824, and Edward, born August 12, 1834. Sumner was a farmer for a time, then taught school in Norfolk, Virginia. Returning to Worcester in 1858, he engaged in the manufacture of valentines. He was listed as being in the wholesale stationery business at 218 Main Street from 1858 until he died on August 29, 1861. His wife, Lura Clark Whitney, then carried on his valentine business from her home on Abbott Street until 1865, at which time she faded from known records.

Edward Whitney became associated with Sumner in 1859, and they were both listed at 218 Main Street, as "Whitney Bros.," until Sumner died. The following year Edward moved to 144 Main Street and was at this location during 1862 and 1863, while George was serving in the army. In 1864 Edward moved to 247 Main Street, and was joined by his brother George C. Whitney within a year. They then advertised under the name of "The Whitney Valentine Co." Edward withdrew from this partnership in 1869 to enter the wholesale stationery and paper business, while George continued manufacturing valentines.

Edward and George maintained the closest sort of business relations all their lives. In fact, their offices adjoined and Edward C. Whitney, George's nephew, told the writer that people would often get into his father's office by mistake, when they were looking for valentines. From 1867 until 1872, George C. Whitney was located at 245 Main Street, while Edward kept the store at 247, then Edward engaged larger quarters at 395 Main Street, and George relocated at 393. Finally, when Edward withdrew from the business, George Whitney went under the name of the "Whitney Manufacturing Co."

Major recognition has been accorded George C. Whitney rather than Edward, understandably, since George engaged in the valentine business, the heart of which was located in Worcester for so many years, while Edward turned to a prosaic trade in wholesale stationery, paper, blank books, paper bags, etc. to which no sentiment could be attached! Early in the 1880's, he moved to 112 Front Street. About this time, he admitted his two sons, Edward Cutting and Sumner Whitney into partnership. Later on he retired, turning his business over to his sons and thereafter spent much of his time in foreign travel.

The statement has been made that George Whitney was a natural designer of valentines. In the beginning he purchased the materials such as lace paper, embossed envelopes, etc., from England, and the colored ornaments or "swags," and cards from Germany, just as Esther Howland did. Thus, it is possible to find valentines with an embossed "Mullord" or "Meek" on the face, of English origin, only to discover the tell-tale small red "W" on the back. Mr. Whitney obviously copied Esther Howland's method of identification. In fact, his early valentines so closely resemble hers that one could not distinguish one from the other if it were not for the Howland "H" and the Whitney "W."

In plate 50 are two Whitney creations of the 1860's. The larger one at the top has a robin's-egg-blue disc with scalloped edge mounted against a larger red one, at the back of the cherub's head. The two perforated gold-and-white medallions in the lower section have vivid blue discs as background. As mentioned in the previous chapter, this method of ornamentation is reported to have been originated by Esther Howland. The other valentine in the same illustration is a dainty gold and white filagree with silver paper, embossed with tiny stars, pasted in back of it, together with four red discs and two dark blue ones. The immediate effect is red, white, and blue set off by delicate gold and silver. Both valentines carry a verse, which is pasted on the inside of the back, titled "Forget-Me-Not," though each has a different rhyme.

In plate 51 are three more Whitney valentines, both produced in the same manner as those just described. They appear to date in the late 1860's.

It was while he was located at 245 Main Street that George Whitney

Plate 50.

Two Whitney valentines, and a T. W. Strong
Valentine Writer.

Plate 51.

Three Whitney valentines of the 1860's.

70

purchased the A. J. Fisher Company of New York, a house said, among other things, to be first responsible for the making of comics commercially, in a really big way. Abraham Fisher was born in 1812, and was engaged in the valentine publishing business in 1835, and perhaps earlier. When Mr. Whitney bought him out, the Fisher concern had some thousands of dollars' worth of cuts and plates for comics on hand in its plant at 24 Vesey Street. Now Mr. Whitney happened to abhor comics. He felt they not only degraded the spirit of St. Valentine's Day, but he did not wish any of his friends and associates to have their feelings wounded, since nearly all were unkind in intent—least of all by a comic from *his* manufactory. His motto was always "Industry, Punctuality, and Christianity."

With the Fisher Company out of the way, Mr. Whitney's next strongest competitor was McLoughlin Brothers, of New York, who also manufactured comics. George Whitney went to see these people and told them of his purchase of all the A. J. Fisher plates and cuts, in connection with their production of comics and of his own dislike for this particular branch of the business. It is not known whether he sold them the Fisher plates or not but being a shrewd Yankee, he doubtless did not make the trip to New York for nothing! It has been recorded that he offered to turn over to them whatever comic business came his way. His own salesmen had never been encouraged to take orders for them but when deemed necessary, they were made up on order, in as limited a way as possible. This stand he adhered to all his life.

His most important purchase was considered to be that of Berlin & Jones, in 1869. This firm was one of the largest manufacturers of valentines in New York and among the oldest. Mr. Berlin was listed as a stationer there in 1850. During 1854-1855 the concern was known as West & Berlin and from 1859-1869 as Berlin & Jones. Many lovely valentines may be encountered by the collector, embossed along the fold in the center, "Lang's Pat. process. Berlin & Jones, Mfrs. N.Y." or else simply "Berlin & Jones." The former inscription is seen more often. Esther Howland bought some of her valentine papers from them, in all likelihood before Mr. Whitney bought them out and moved the business to Worcester.

As a demand for greater production grew, George Whitney required more space, so he moved to 393 Main Street, in 1874, where he remained for eight years. With the ever increasing volume of business, Mr. Whitney decided there must be some way of making valentine materials domestically to avoid imports. In fact, he concluded these materials could be manufactured here just as well and probably better. It was not long before the best possible machinery he could purchase for embossing and making paper lace was installed—giant double-cylinder presses together with all the other necessary appurtenances for a large valentine factory.

The exact date of Mr. Whitney's purchase of Miss Howland's and Mr. Taft's valentine business is not known. The New England Valentine Co. business heading appears for the last time in the Worcester directory in 1880, as at 425 Main Street. According to a statement made at the time of Mr. Whitney's death in 1915, "The Taft and Howland stock, together·with that of the Bullard Art Publishing Co.,[1] came into the possession of Mr. Whitney in *due course of time.*" It is such vague generalities as these that make the task of a researcher so difficult. In any event, before 1888, George C. Whitney had bought out eight or ten of his competitors, some of them apparently being little-known companies. His business was devoted entirely to valentines until 1876, at which time all sorts of other specialties were gradually introduced, such as Christmas, New Year's, and Easter cards, calendars, and various kinds of booklets.

Another interesting angle of Whitney's affairs was the *verse* department. The writing of sentimental rhymes for valentines was one more method of money-making for a vast army of scribes from all over the United States. Effusions honoring St. Valentine poured into their offices at such a rate that Whitney's mail pile became quite something for the post office to reckon with!

From 393 Main Street, the Whitney plant moved to the Taylor Building at 184 Front Street. The business developed such an enormous volume so rapidly that in 1883, Mr. Taylor built another story to the building. They were located there for nearly ten years. While there, the firm was incorporated as the George C. Whitney Co., with Mr. Whitney as president. In time even these quarters grew too crowded, and it was then that Mr. Whitney leased the last home of the industry at 67 Union Street. It was at this Union Street location that a disastrous fire occurred on January 12, 1910.

At the time it took place, the firm had $200,000 worth of stock in trade and $100,000 worth of machinery, most of which was totally destroyed. Included among the machinery were eight presses of the largest pattern used for printing and color work. They weighed six tons each.

When the fire broke out, about nine o'clock in the evening, there were seventy men working, as there had been every night, completing orders in time for St. Valentine's Day. George C. Whitney's son, Warren, and his wife, were on the fifth floor in the building inspecting some of the new valentines, when the watchman sounded the fire alarm. The blaze spread so rapidly that Mr. Whitney encountered considerable difficulty leading his wife through the dense smoke into the street to safety. Ap-

[1] The Bullard Art Publishing Company was in business in Worcester during 1887-1888 and then moved to Springfield, Massachusetts.

Two Whitney valentines and envelope of the
1870's.

Plate 52.

Plate 53.

Berlin & Jones valentines of the 1850's.

74

proximately thirty thousand people were attracted by the enormous fire, which was said to resemble a volcano. Explosions were frequent, and at times showers of burning valentines would be thrown high in the air. An estimated $60,000 of valentine stock was ready for shipment, with an equal amount in Easter favors, and all were a total loss. Fortunately, 80 per cent of the valentine orders had long since been shipped, to all parts of the United States.

Two days later President George C. Whitney let the contract for a temporary roof over the part of the plant not wholly gutted with the expectation that seventy-five men would be back at work within a few days. Mr. Whitney had been leasing this property but he now bought it and had a modern six-story building erected. Once the building had been completed, they employed upward of 450 hands, and occupied 75,000 feet of floor space.

Prior to our engagement in World War I, or about 1915, the valentines produced at this Union Street plant ranged in retail price from one dollar to fifty dollars, but there finally developed a lack of interest in the immense, satin-padded varieties that were so costly. Possibly the outraged spirit of the thrifty miss of Esther Howland's time who dismissed her suitor for being so extravagant as to buy her a ten-dollar May basket, held council with St. Valentine in the Great Beyond and they concluded to put a blight on such wasteful ways! At any rate, in the later 1920's the most expensive valentine Whitney's made retailed at less than five dollars. The George C. Whitney Company had grown into a tremendous business, with offices located in New York, Boston, and Chicago.

George C. Whitney continued to be active in the concern until two years before his death on November 7, 1915, and then his interests passed into the hands of a son, Warren A. Whitney. When it was finally decided to liquidate the firm on February 27, 1942, there were 176 employees, some of whom had worked for the company for more than thirty years. Mr. Whitney regretted closing down a business that had been in operation in one family continuously for seventy-seven years, but the critical paper shortage, together with other restrictions that were imposed due to the war, made it necessary. Their presses, stock on hand, and good will were sold to a company in Chicago specializing in color printing and the business property disposed of to a Worcester concern. Most of the old plates from which the valentines were printed were lost in the fire. Plates of the later valentines were scrapped from time to time, as styles changed, so that none of the old ones are in existence. And so ended the saga of the valentine business in Worcester, starting with Esther Howland in 1849 and ending with the George C. Whitney Company in 1942—almost a century had been replete with beautiful sentiment!

VI

COMIC VALENTINES

BENEATH THE POLITELY SWEET exterior of the sentimental valentine, there lurked an amazingly different type of valentine, the comic. Sharp in caricature and sometimes venomous in humor, it lampooned schoolteachers, the skinny, the fat, the smug, the conceited, and the dandy, mincing no words. The comic valentine was a masterpiece of the grotesque, with barbed verse and unflattering color, far from sentimental, expressing everything but love.

It seems highly probable that what are popularly known as "comics" today but termed "caricatures" originally were abroad in our country earlier than we had supposed. A Valentine Writer, published by W. Borradaile of New York, in May 1823, contains several verses for use with "caricatures," indicating that comics were in vogue at this early date. Undoubtedly many were made by hand, either in pen and ink, or water color. It is not presuming too much to believe that the last quarter of the eighteenth century also saw its quota of these scurrilous missives. The early political caricatures of William Charles must have inspired certain engravers and printers to publish comics, but any prior to 1830 would be very rare indeed. However, by 1840 comic valentines were produced on a relatively large scale commercially and have been much in evidence ever since. They are typical of their times and no collection is complete without a few representatives.

While some of the earliest were lithographed and hand colored, wood blocks were soon used extensively; in fact, more so as time went on than were any other processes. Those taken from wood blocks were at first colored by hand, generally in a crude manner. Later, while they were still being utilized, colors were achieved by second and third printings. An amusing advertisement of all sorts of valentines dating about 1850 is illustrated in plate 54.

Among the earliest New York publishers of comics, known to have been making them prior to 1840, were Elton & Company and A. J. Fisher. Robert H. Elton was doing business in New York in 1833 and possibly

Plate 54.

Valentine advertisement, c. 1850.

Plate 55.

Early comic by Elton & Company, New York.

earlier. He claimed to have published valentines in 1834. One of his comics is shown in plate 55, and chapter III displays two of his lithographs. During 1849 he advertised valentines from his store at 18 Division Street. Sometime after 1855 he sold out to McLoughlin Brothers. During his time he published all sorts of booklets, and advertised the following in 1843:

"Song Books, of every variety and description, comic, sentimental, patriotic, negro, naval, Irish, Scotch, English, Temperance, and Bachanalian, from 6 to 25 cents each. Also, Dream Books, Fortune Tellers, Letter Writers, etc."

Another of his advertisements, also in 1843, carried a woodcut of a chubby winged cupid reposing on a cushion. It read:

"Valentines! Valentines! Hear ye! Hear ye! All you forlorn damsels and bashful bachelors, you are hereby notified to repair in due season to

Elton's, 98 Nassau St.

Plate 56.

Comic by Turner & Fisher, dated 1847.

78

Plate 57.

Comic by A. J.
Fisher, New York.

LADY KILLER.
With bow and smirk, and hop and jerk,
The Lady-Killing elf,
Will find at last when time has pass'd,
He's only kill'd himself.

A. J. Fisher, New York.

and then and there procure one of his delicious love letters, with their beautiful colored embellishments, and having added a delicate sentiment of your own, seal and direct the same to the dear object of your affections, thereby laying the foundation of the most true of all earthly happiness, viz matrimony.

Elton has a few comical valentines to be sent to fusty old bachelors and sour old maids that are beyond cure. Also, a general assortment of Valentine Writers."

While Elton made a specialty of publishing valentines, he sold all sorts of other objects, from quill pens to fancy playing cards, sealing wax, and took commissions for executing wood engravings. He also published *The Washingtonian Temperance Almanac* consisting of sixty-four pages. So in his business career, he turned out a vast amount of material.

A. J. Fisher's history is outlined more fully in the chapter devoted to lithographs. He was a prodigious workman, apparently dealing with asso-

79

Plate 58.

An early comic by
T. W. Strong, New
York.

Plate 60.

Charles P. Huestis
comic of the 1840's.

Plate 59.

T. W. Strong comic,
dated 1849.

ciates off and on, who may have assisted him with his several branches, located in Boston, Baltimore, and Philadelphia, besides his main office in New York. He was listed over the years under various firm names, such as Fisher & Bro., Turner & Fisher, Fisher & Dennison, but he finally signed officially as A. J. Fisher. He was in business from the early 1830's until he sold out to George C. Whitney, after nearly forty years spent as a wholesaler and retailer, publisher, bookseller, and stationer. At the time Fisher sold out he was known as the largest publisher of comics in the business. A Turner & Fisher comic, dated February 12, 1847 and mailed from Charlestown, Massachusetts, is shown in plate 56. This is a double sheet, in which form some of the earlier comics may sometimes be encountered. An A. J. Fisher, undated but probably of the 1860's may be seen in plate 57.

Starting in 1842, Thomas W. Strong of New York became one of the best-known publishers and importers of valentines of all sorts. He made up various types of assortments for the trade, some selling at anywhere from $1000 to $5000 per lot. To tell more of his history here would only repeat that discussed in chapter III. One of his early comics, taken from a woodcut, is illustrated in plate 58. Many caricatures were devoted to the subject of intemperance during this period. Another T. W. Strong, circa 1849, is shown in plate 59. This one lampoons the "Opera Belle." She is seen wearing a huge pin featuring a young man. The artist was in no way neglectful when he sketched a peacock on her fan! This was sent from Southbridge, Massachusetts, February 13, 1849.

A name contemporaneous with that of T. W. Strong was Charles P. Huestis of 104 Nassau Street, New York. An example of his work is shown in plate 60, which dated in the early 1840's. In some directories Huestis is listed from 1842 until 1853. Apparently he was responsible for a good many comics but little is known of his activities.

T. Frere published the hand-colored woodcut, "To a Drunkard" in plate 61. He advertised as an engraver and publisher, of 84 Nassau Street, New York, where he was located between 1852-1855, and perhaps longer. Since every publisher of comics lampooned those who imbibed to excess, it is interesting to examine one of the accompanying rhymes. "To a Drunkard" reads thus:

"Oh! horrid, frightful, stupid drunkard,
    Receptacle of gin and beer,
    If e'er you pester me with nonsense,
    My answer shall be simply, 'clear.' "

Charles Magnus was located at 12 Frankfort Street, New York, between 1854 and 1870. Like Frere, his name is not particularly well known among collectors, so in all likelihood he did not direct much of his efforts toward valentines. A colored lithographed mechanical,[1] in the way of a comic by Magnus is illustrated in plate 62, dedicated to "The Home Guard." A tongue of paper is attached to a movable part of the top of the head, so that it waggles up and down, when pulled. This perhaps dates at the time of the Civil War in the early 1860's. Sometimes his valentines are marked "Chas. Magnus" together with his address but others may only carry "12 Frankfort St., N. Y."

James Wrigley was a fairly prolific contributor to the field of valentines. He was located in New York, between 1846 and 1870, at 27 Chatham Street, and also at 394 Grand Street. One of his comics is shown in plate 62.

One of the earliest caricatures illustrated in the book is the hand-colored wood engraving pictured in plate 63. Neither the artist nor the publisher are known. It is the oldest of this type in the author's collection and is so quaint, despite the fact that it is both crude and ludicrous, that it is an interesting example which may well date prior to 1840.

Of particular interest to New England is "The Pride of the Mills" in plate 64. Various details permit the assumption that this is a caricature

[1] A valentine card with moving figures is called a mechanical.

TO A DRUNKARD.

Oh ! horrid, frightful, stupid drunkard,
Receptacle of gin and beer,
If e'er you pester me with nonsense,
My answer shall be simply, "clear !"

T. Frere, Printer, Engraver and Publisher, 84 Nassau St., N.Y.

Plate 61.

Comic by T. Frere,
New York.

Norcross, New York

Plate 62.

Left: Mechanical comic by Charles Magnus, New York. *Right:* A James Wrigley comic, New York.

83

of Lucy Larcom, who worked as a girl in the "Merimac" Mills at Lowell, Massachusetts, and was later distinguished as a writer and teacher. Over her shoulder, it will be noted, she displays a copy of the *Lowell Offering*, a remarkable little magazine written, edited, and published under varying names from 1840-1846, by the women employees. During this period, these workers were mostly old American stock, and their employment was an innovation.

The verse under the print reads:

"The Pride of the Mills"
"At Loom, at the spindle, in parlor, at pen,
So ably each station she fills;
She's the envy of maidens—the idol of men,
As they point to the 'Pride of the Mills.' "

Whoever was responsible for this "offering" is not known.

A rare Civil War item in the way of a caustic comic emanated from Richmond, Virginia, and was published by George Dunn & Company in 1864. It is pictured in plate 65. Comics of this type were often sent unsigned as they carry extremely uncomplimentary verses. It reads:

A woman of ill-temper,
Fades quickly away
Let her always remember,
A second wife is gay.

Plate 63.

An early wood engraving.

Author's Collection

THE PRIDE OF THE MILLS.

At loom, at the spindle, in parlor, at pen,
So ably each station she fills;
She's the envy of maidens—the idol of men,
As they point to the "Pride of the Mills."

Plate 64.

Lucy Larcom, Pride of the "Merimac" (Mass.) Mills.

American Antiquarian Society

Plate 65.

Civil War caricature, by George Dunn & Company, Rich-mond, Virginia.

Norcross, New York

Plate 66.

Soldier, by New
York Union Valen-
tine Company.

Norcross, New York

"Anathema on him who screws and hoards,
Who robs the poor of wheat, potatoes, bread;
On all his gains may withering blights descend—
On body, bones, on intellect and head."

This seemingly has more political implications than satire, it is so replete
with bitterness!

Two especially interesting valentines published by the New York
Union Valentine Company, of 134 William Street, may be seen in plates
66 and 67. The first, a hand-colored woodcut, is to a "Soldier" and the
rhyme runs:

"You are a gallant soldier,
With a splendid figure for parade;
The country is safe in your keeping,
So long as you fight in the shade.

I fancy myself *your* beloved!
Wouldn't you have a jolly good time?
I'd make you stand guard over a cradle,
And do double duty to valentine."

86

The two ladies in the background looking him over are not so impressed as he thinks!

The hand-colored lithograph in plate 67 is especially interesting because it is very seldom one finds a comic with an embossed border. As such, they sold for so little that they were gotten up in the cheapest possible manner. The verse under this one is amusing, too. It goes like this:

"Over the tub is a good place to learn
The virtue of your station,
Over the tub is a good place to earn
An industrious reputation.
Just rub away and in good time,
You'll wash the shirt of valentine."

The recipient of this valentine was apparently expected to have something to look forward to!

Very little is known about the N. Y. Union Valentine Co., as they identified themselves, but they were undoubtedly in business during the 1860's. An "American Valentine Co." was listed at 165 William Street in 1863. They advertised "Soldier valentine packets, Army valentine packets, New Military comic valentines, Torch of Love packets," etc. Also adver-

Norcross, New York

Plate 67.

Unusual comic printed on embossed paper, by New York Union Valentine Company.

tised was a "N. Y. Valentine Corner" at 134 William Street. Time will possibly throw more light on these concerns.

A well-known manufacturer of comics was McLoughlin Brothers of New York. Many of their valentines were downright cruel, as may be seen in plate 68. However, most of them were more apt to be on the order of "Spooney" (plate 69). This firm began publishing valentines in 1848 and like T. W. Strong, Elton, and others, carried them along with toy books and all sorts of paper novelties. Most of their comics were produced from wood blocks, with the color achieved from second and third printings, the shades in most general use being red, green, blue, and yellow. The basic woodcut and verse were printed in black. Valentines of this kind were produced in sheets of sixteen and then cut apart after they were completed.

According to a note from Carl Drepperd, McLoughlin Brothers moved to Springfield, Massachusetts, about 1940. They had stored in the basement of their warehouse their priceless stock of original company catalogues, sample books of all their old valentines, etc., which were ruined when a flood inundated the place. Considering the fact that this firm was one hundred years old, it meant a serious loss to them, not only from

GONE TO SEED.

Plate 68.

A cruel comic, by McLoughlin Brothers, New York.

Author's Collection

88

SPOONEY.

Sweet maiden, with the love-sick eyes,
And face pale as the moon,
The man who draws you for a prize
Need never buy a spoon.
McLOUGHLIN BROS. Manuf. N. Y.

Plate 69.

"Spooney" by Mc-
Loughlin Brothers,
New York.

the financial angle but also the sentimental. Few concerns are operating today who were in business a century ago. It certainly would have been interesting to examine the books of sample valentines dating from 1848!

Perhaps the most revealing and accurate account of the valentine trade in this country during the 1850's may be derived from an interview given many years ago by Mr. Phillip J. Cozans, a large valentine manufacturer in New York from approximately 1850 until 1862. According to him, valentines did not become popular in the United States before 1840 and at this time so-called cheap valentines were actually high priced, the ordinary colored comics being sold at twenty-five to fifty cents. The expensive truly sentimental valentines were not then made here commercially. However, the notion soon gained acceptance and the demand increased so rapidly that the manufacturers were then able, with their expanded operations, to reduce prices, and bring the cards into almost universal exchange. According to Mr. Cozans, over three million valentines, ranging in retail price from three cents to thirty dollars, were sold in 1847. The race in sales was almost equally divided between "comics" and "sentimentals," though the latter outvalued the comics considerably. The sales for 1857 amounted to over a quarter of a million dollars, exclusive of the materials utilized in making them, which if also counted would bring the total to three hundred thousand. Mr. Cozans remarked that this was "a vast sum to be expended in the idle gratification of what has, somehow, become a national whim." By 1858, the capital invested in the business here in the United States amounted to around seventy thousand dollars.

Imported valentines were not popular, according to Mr. Cozans. Many of the mechanicals were brought from England, but even these ingenious contrivances did not meet with approval here. Apparently our idea of a joke differed from that of our cousin, John Bull. About ten thousand dollars' worth of valentines were imported in 1857, but the venture was not a commercial success. Apparently the impact of our "American made" was then being felt as the following advertisement appeared in the *Boston Transcript* of February 9, 1847:

"English Valentines, Per *Hibernia*.

A. S. Jordan, No. 2 Milk Street, respectfully informs his friends that he has just received by the above steamer, the greatest assortment of Valentines to be found in Cupid's regions, among which may be found the following kinds: Comic, Sentimental, Lovesick, Acrostic, Funny, Burlesque, Curious, Characteristic, Humorous, Beautiful, Heart-struck, Witty, Arabesque, Courting, Serio-Comical, Bewitching, Poetical, Heart-rending, Love-encouraging, Trifling, Caricature, Heart-piercing, Serio-tragical, Laughable, Silly, Spiteful, Original, Enlivening, Heart-aching, Despairing, Raving-mad, Heart-killing, High-flown, Lampooning, Romantic, Look-out, Proposal, Espousal, Matrimonial, Hen-pecking, Suicidal, and many other varieties. Wholesale buyers would do well to call before purchasing elsewhere, as the selection has been made by one of the first London houses engaged in that particular business."

During the 1850's and possibly earlier, St. Valentine's Day was made an occasion by some youths for playing anonymous practical jokes. Before the day of prepaying postage was inaugurated, rival lovers sometimes victimized each other. One trick was to send each other a bulky parcel, duly directed in mock feminine hand, as coming from the disputed lady. The package was slyly committed to the postmaster, who took care to levy sufficient postage on the unlucky recipient, whose curiosity was bound to overcome his cupidity. Exaggerated caricatures replaced the heavier parcels in due course of time.

Magazines usually aimed some jibes at Cupid each February 14. In 1871 *Harper's Bazaar* published a cartoon of a maiden walking in the park with two joined hearts on her ermine muff, and a bow and arrow perched on her fetching bonnet, "with a ribbon and a feather and a bit of lace upon it."

THE FLORIST

O. Hodgson. 10. Cloth Fair.

Plate 70.

"The Florist," by Francesco Bartolozzi, the
famous eighteenth-century stipple engraver.

91

In England, as in this country, the earliest comic valentines were devoted to caricatures of people or were directed at various trades, and as such were reflective of the times. Famous artists engaged in executing political caricatures apparently could not resist doing a number of valentines as well. In America, during the eighteenth or early part of the nineteenth century, there were no artists of repute comparable to Francesco Bartolozzi, George and Robert Cruikshank, Alfred Crowquill, the Corboulds, and Heath. Their work in valentines followed a different pattern, and their sense of humor was not only different, but subtler. The contrast is so sharp that a few English examples are being shown, as a matter of interest.

Francesco Bartolozzi (1727-1815) was born in Florence, Italy, where he studied art in his youth, later being apprenticed to John Wagner, an engraver in Venice. He went to England in 1764 as "Engraver to the King," and later became one of the original members of the Royal Academy. Plate 70 displays a piece of his work, titled "The Florist." This is actually more fanciful than caricature, though apparently aimed at the florists' trade, since a greenhouse may be seen in the background. This valentine, a hand-colored engraving, appears to be an adaptation from an original, though very likely it was made from the original plate. It was published by O. Hodgson, 10, Cloth Fair. Bartolozzi's "Sailor's Farewell," probably his most famous valentine, is shown in plate 86.

An engraved valentine by an unknown artist that might date back to the 1830's is illustrated in plate 71. This is an excellent example of English humor, in no way subtle! The verse reads:

> "Ods bobs, I'll never wed with you,
> And leave my rosy smiling Sue,
> With all thy pelf, thou shan't be mine,
> Thou ugly wrinkled valentine."

During the 1840's a considerable number of comic valentines displaying a more commercial air appeared in England, simultaneously with those produced here, though still of a different nature. Among the most prominent makers was A. Park of 41 Leonard Street, London. He initiated among others, a series representing men with insect bodies. J. & F. Harwood of Fenchurch Street published a number also, a notable example being one of a lady with a parrot's head (plate 72). The artist's name is not quite legible. The verse beneath the damsel reads:

> "Hah! Hah! Old chatterbox, I have you now;
> You are daguerreotyped, so like, I vow.
> Thou whisperer of slander! death to truth!
> Destroyer of the hopes and joys of youth!

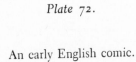

Ods bobs, I'll never wed with you,
And leave my rosy smiling Sue,
With all thy pelf, thou shant be mine,
Thou ugly wrinkled Valentine

Plate 71.

**An amusing comic
by an early English
engraver.**

Norcross, New York

Plate 72.

An early English comic.

93

A tailor makes him ! 'tis most apt and true,
And doth apply most faithfully to you :
Behold your likeness at the tailor's door,
Unlike you, silent—therefore less a bore.

The coat fits well the covering of wood ;
The case is yours, the simile holds good.
" He has no head !"—You have me there, you say.
" No more have you :—'tis equal every way."

Plate 73.

An early English comic, unsigned but probably
by Alfred Crowquill.

94

With innuendos and a pitying sigh,
You blast fair fame, yet hardly tell a lie:
Caressing falsehood—everybody's friend—
You triumph now,—but wait and see the end."

Along with the series of men with insect bodies, women with the heads of birds, Elliot of Holywell Street produced a series in which ladies composed of fruit, flowers, or vegetables were quite attractive, so that this type of valentine must have been popular at a fairly early date.

Plate 73 shows another comic thought to be from the hand of Alfred Crowquill. It was published by Maurice & Company and lampoons the dude. It is well executed, with a handsomely engraved border unlike any produced here. The verse accompanying this valentine was calculated to make the recipient most unhappy. It reads:

"A tailor makes him! 'tis most apt and true,
And doth apply most faithfully to you:
Behold your likeness at the tailor's door,
Unlike you, silent—therefore less a bore.

The coat fits well the covering of wood;
The case is yours, the simile holds good.
'He has no head!'—You have me there, you say.
'No more have you:—'tis equal every way.'"

During the 1850's comic and often vulgar caricatures were produced in substantial quantity in England. A large number were intended as skits on various trades and were often issued in a series. Some were humorous portraits of various tradesmen, such as blacksmiths, cheesemongers, candlemakers, staymakers, etc. Some others, rather sketchily drawn, appeared by S. T. Wood, of 268 Strand, while another series carrying considerable detail may be encountered bearing the initials R. Y.

Among other well-known English publishers of comics were J. L. Marks, who perpetrated a series of rather vulgar caricatures during the early 1840's; R. Carr, of Houndsditch; G. Gilbert; Elliot, of Holywell Street; G. Ingram, City Road; Rock & Company; Pickering & Company; E. Lloyd; and J. Simmons & Company, all known to have been producing many comics during the 1860's.

Comic valentines flourish to this day in the United States but they are not so much in evidence as formerly. Today they consist of a single sheet displaying a broad cartoon, flamboyantly colored, usually with an abusive verse below.

VII

LATE VICTORIAN VALENTINES

WHILE A GENERAL DECLINE in taste gradually became apparent during the 1860's, as a growing population and consequent wealth and sophistication increased in America, still all the valentines produced during the following decades were not entirely "bad." The rapid transition from "handwork" to "machine made" was attended by many changes of note. We were depending less and less on foreign imports. Therefore, in tracing the history of valentines in this country it would be a serious omission not to paint the entire picture through the 1880's, and onward to the turn of the century.

Progress in the field of lithography went on apace, and so we were soon manufacturing the ornamental boxes designed to contain the decorative built-up valentines, which we had formerly purchased from England and France. An excellent example of one of these boxes, together with its original valentine in a shadow-box effect, is shown in plate 74. While it will be noted that the lace paper is coarse, at least the effect as a whole is both quaint and attractive. Plate 75 illustrates another of the boxed valentines, again showing the box cover, together with the pretty valentine it contained. The paper lace which framed the face in the center medallion is in gold and white. The coloring in the lithographs of this period, the 1870's and 1880's, was rich and deep. Any collector would do well to add a few of these shadow boxes to his collection though they are not altogether easy to find today, particularly in a good state of preservation.

A sweet bit of Victorian fancy is revealed in the valentine dance program also shown in plate 75. This is laid flat so that the front and back of the cover may be seen. The cover has a fluff of white chiffon, with a hand made of wax mounted in the center. A tiny blue velvet bow is tied about the wrist. The border of the program is perforated lace in gold and white, and a silk cord and tassel is attached to mark the program, which includes popular dances of the period, such as the lanciers, quadrille, redowa, and schottische, with a few waltzes interspersed. This is dated 1878.

Plate 74. Shadow-box valentine and cover of the 1870's.

Cover of the 1870's.

Shadow-box valentine.

Plate 75.

Valentine dance program dated 1878.

Author's Collection

An extravagant piece of Victorianism of the 1880's in the form of a miniature valentine fire screen (plate 76) was produced for the swain who could afford to indulge his sweetheart to the tune of fifty "1880" dollars! The center is heavily embossed paper, edged with real lace! Mementos of this kind are rarely encountered today. The manufacturer undoubtedly did not produce many of them as customers in this price range would hardly be plentiful!

During the 1890's, valentines were all basically more or less of the same general style. They consisted of a double sheet, the face or top being heavily and coarsely embossed in color, with a verse printed on the inside page. The more expensive valentines would have two layers above the face, as shown by the example in plate 77. The second layer of this specimen is lithographed with carnations in the center, and roses on the border.

Plate 76.

Miniature fire screen valentine of the 1880's.

99

Plate 77.

Valentine of the Gay Nineties.

Plate 78.

A child's valentine,
c. 1900.

Plate 79.

A valentine wall
hanging, c. 1900.

Plate 80. A table model valentine, c. 1900.

Norcross,
New York

GREET THEE!   VALENTINE.

101

Courtesy of Mrs. W. S. Curtis

Plate 81. Pink crab apple blossoms encircle a blue satin
center in this valentine, c. 1900.

Above the lithograph is a layer of white lace, outlined here and there in
silver and decorated with swags, such as the figures in the center and the
roses in each corner, which lent color. The run-of-the-mill valentine made
to sell at from five to ten cents each, produced from the early 1900's, consisted of the double sheet as described, with one layer of coarse lace over
the embossed face. These spelled the death knell for paper-lace valentines. It seemed a sad ending for the earlier beautiful copies of fine real
lace. Instead of the machine age producing bigger and better materials,

Plate 82.   German mechanical valentine of the early 1900's.

Plate 83.   A group of German mechanical valentines, early 1900's.

they became cheaper and coarser. Thus, a change does not always connote improvement.

At the turn of the century came a marked change in valentine styles. With the decline and fall of paper lace, there emerged lithographed novelties reminiscent of Louis Prang. Many of these novelties were preferable to the coarsened lace product, and some displayed a certain amount of charm. Plate 78 shows a lithographed paper fan for children, the medallion carrying a verse for each day of the week. Other novelties followed, such as wall hangings, like the one pictured in plate 79. It will be noted that children are featured, a decided departure from earlier days! Other valentines during this era featured a cardboard rest, so that they might be displayed on a table or mantel, such as the one shown in plate 80. Many of the lithographed novelties of this age will be considered highly collectible items in years to come, particularly one as handsome as the heart formed of crab apple blossoms, encircling a blue satin center, shown in plate 81.

Plate 84.

A valentine from
World War I.

This Valentine is just to tell
That in my mind you ever dwell
And here at home or "over there"
My thoughts go with you everywhere

Plate 85.

A valentine from
World War II.

The machine age brought with it mounting labor costs, so our shores were soon flooded with foreign goods which could be brought in at less cost than we could produce them for ourselves. From Germany came a series of ingenious contrivances in the way of mechanical valentines. Plates 82 and 83 display several of these so-called "pull-outs." They actually did pull out and then stand up! These brightly colored chromo-lithographs were made in any number of sizes and shapes, and added a distinct flavor to our own slightly jaded valentine market. Many collectors today are adding these German products to their collections for they represent a distinct phase in valentine art.

In closing the story of American valentines, it seems appropriate at this time to remember that the men in our Armed Services have always had their valentines, too. Plates 84 and 85 display examples made for World War I and World War II. We trust these will end that series!

PART TWO

(Author's Collection)

Theorem valentine by Amanda Snowball, dated 1849,
American. (See also pages 32 and 33.)

Hand-colored lithograph by A. Park, London, c. 1860.
(See also page 126.)

Valentine by Joseph Mansell with his famous perforated
and gilded lace border. English, c. 1850. (See also pages
136 to 158.)

(Norcross, New York)

Valentine by Addenbrooke with perforated lace border.
English, c. 1850. (See also pages 172 to 174.)

VIII

ENGLISH VALENTINE HISTORY:
ENGRAVINGS AND LITHOGRAPHS

WHEREAS THE HISTORY OF the custom of celebrating St. Valentine's Day in America was a comparatively simple event from the very beginning, concerning itself chiefly with sentiment and love, such was not the case in merrie old England. While the early Roman custom of drawing lots, which was taken over by the English and Scots, to see who should be their valentines, was also followed in this country during the eighteenth century, none of the other English superstitions or rituals were observed here, so far as can be ascertained.

The alliance of young people on February 14 and the superstition that birds selected their mates on the same day was followed in England during the sixteenth and seventeenth centuries by the bestowal of gifts. That this custom often ran into considerable expense is revealed by that fabulous diarist, Samuel Pepys, who in 1667 stated that the Duke of York, being drawn as valentine to Lady Arabella Stuart, "did give her a ring about £800." Lord North, in 1645, severely censured the habit as "costly and idle—which by tacit generale consent wee lay down as obsolete." However, it is revealed that on February 14, 1661, Sir William Batten sent Mrs. Pepys "half a dozen pairs of gloves, a pair of silk stockings and garters." In the *Diary of a Country Parson*, February 14, 1782, the Rev. James Woodforde notes, "this being Valentine's Day gave 52 children of this Parish as usual 1 penny each."

An early English superstition associated with St. Valentine's Day was to the effect that the first man seen by a woman on that day was destined to be her future spouse. An amusing story was related in *The Connoisseur* of 1754, when a young lady of that period wrote on St. Valentine's Eve, "I got five bay leaves and pinned four of them to the corners of my pillow and the fifth to the middle and then I dremt of my sweetheart. Betty said we should be married before the year was out. But to make more sure I boiled an egg hard and took out the yolk and filled it with salt, and when I went to bed ate it, shell and all, without speaking or drinking." She concluded, "Would you think it? Mr. Blossom is my man.

I lay a-bed and shut my eyes all morning till he came to our house for I would not have seen another man before him for all the world."

Some humorous tales have been told of other lovesick damsels who remained in bed, with tight-closed eyes, until they felt sure that the hour was nigh when an admired swain would pass by. Then they would arise, bedeck themselves in their best and make for a conspicuous window.

In Shakespeare's time the valentine greeting was "Good morrow, 'tis St. Valentine's Day." It is claimed that the man or maid who repeated it first on meeting a person of the opposite sex received a present! In Scotland they had other ideas. The first youth or girl one met by chance on Valentine's Day became their valentine. Doubtless there was more than one way of getting around this superstition, in case the wrong one came along. There was no law against closing their eyes and not opening them again until the right one was in sight!

In rural England there was yet another quaint custom. The young girls were wont to go to their churchyard late at night, singing songs of invitation to their sweethearts to come and fetch them at the stroke of midnight. They ran about knocking on doors, ringing bells and having a hilarious time, while younger children were known to sing:

> "Curl your locks as I do mine
> Two before and three behind
> So Good Morning, valentine.
> Hurra! Hurra! Hurra!"

Few if any of such superstitions were practiced in America, but the custom of sending messages of love or sentiment on St. Valentine's Day has persisted over the few centuries of our existence and today is still a matter of hearts and flowers.

Some of the first English valentines began, as they did in America, as sheets of paper with verses written upon them and no decoration other than that the ink, as well as the paper, was sometimes in color. The earliest known valentine, dated 1415, was a message written by Charles, Duke of Orleans, while he was imprisoned in the Tower of London. This was preserved in the British Museum. Another one of the earliest valentines was written by the poet John Lydgate, in praise of Catherine, wife of Henry V, also during the fifteenth century.

Commercial valentines began in England when well-known print-makers started to issue either sentimental or humorous illustrations combined with verses. Many types were made, some decorated but with blank spaces so the purchaser could fill them in with his own verse. These were sold by "Fancy Stationers." The greatest single commercial advance came about with the advent of engravings, woodcuts, and lithographs.

Plate 86.

"The Sailor's Farewell," hand-colored copperplate engraving by Francesco Bartolozzi.

111

Plate 87.

Early copperplate engraving.

112

Since the English were fairly glorying in their antiquity before this nation was born, it is not surprising that they were busy making valentines from the time love missives were conceived. It is, therefore, possible to illustrate graphically the growth of the custom of sending valentines from among an immense store of English productions to be found in this country. As might also be expected, the English collectors, such as Jonathan King and Andrew Teur, kept records, which is something we have not always been too careful about in the past.

Andrew Teur, a man who gained recognition both as a printer and publisher, and as the author of the life of Bartolozzi, the engraver, cultivated some interesting collections, including valentines. The Teur collection was devoted largely to hand-colored engravings and lithographs dating between 1822 and 1850. He was also fortunate enough to own a number of the artist's preliminary sketches, usually done in a monochrome water-color wash, though some were in ink, or in sepia paint. His collection also stressed the transition from copperplate engravings to lithographs, both of which were hand colored. Among the prominent artists and engravers of this period were the Cruikshanks (George and Robert), Corbould, Read, and Heath, the last named was employed by Acker and acknowledged to be "a comic artist of repute." The valentines by these artists dated largely from 1822 to 1832 and were both of a sentimental nature and comic. They were dominated by the skill of the engraving combined with a fine sense of coloring. There was one series of trade valentines devoted to such subjects as the hatter, the milkman, the chandler, the cheesemonger, etc., that were typical of their times.

With the customary English thoroughness, Teur acquired his collection of valentines from the original stock of printers and merchants, and so it contained a large series of patterns and proofs. He recorded opposite each valentine the date of production, the number of copies sold each year in color or monochrome, if or when the valentine was embossed or "laced," with comments in some cases to the effect that the watermark was of such a date but that the plate was used ten years earlier. Of particular value were his notations giving the name of the designer or engraver, with an occasional brief biography, such information being highly prized by serious collectors.

One of the most charming of the early valentines shown here is "The Sailor's Farewell" (plate 86) by the famous Italian stipple engraver, Francesco Bartolozzi, who lived in England for some years and became a Royal Academician. It was taken from a copperplate engraving and hand colored. Another by him is in the style of "the endless knot of love," of which there are numerous variations by other artists, either hand painted or lithographed.

Plate 87 illustrates another valentine of about the same period, taken

Plate 88.

Original valentine
sketch by George
Corbould, c. 1819.

from a copperplate engraving. The workmanship of this unknown artist
is by no means as skillful as Bartolozzi's but reflects the style of this era.

An original valentine sketch by the eminent artist, George Corbould,
is shown in plate 88. The border design is in pen and ink and the charming center medallion, in water color. So far as is known, the verse was
penned by the artist, and reads:

> "The Lamb, the letter, and the dove,
> We own are emblems true:
> Peace, tenderness, dear Nymph, and Love,
> Must always dwell with you."

This sketch is thought to date about 1819.

The lady wearing the exaggerated hat in plate 89 appears to be the
work of Robert Cruikshank, as it is closely similar to his "Aging Lover,"
dated 1825. The lines in the engraving are strong and firm, showing to
advantage the writing at the base, which reads:

"From dulling rain alike and Solar heat,
    Your hat affords me a secure retreat,
    Accept, Dear Girl, this loving heart of mine,
    And be my fashionable valentine."

Events of the times were sometimes portrayed in valentines, as was the visitation of Halley's Comet in 1835. The charming design shown in plate 90 was originally from a copperplate engraving but later on reprints were made in lithographs. Apparently it proved to be a popular subject—recurring again with the next appearance of the comet in 1910.

Plate 89.   Caricature "Fashionable Valentine" by Robert Cruikshank.

The interesting valentine by the well-known illustrator and painter, Kenny Meadows, (plate 91) dated 1832, is an uncolored lithograph. This appeared first in an engraving, and later as a hand-colored lithograph by Lloyd. Whether Meadows ever did other valentine designs the writer has been unable to learn. The one shown is imbued with so much simple artistic merit that it is hoped others by him may come to light. Another valentine similar in its general style is pictured in plate 92. It is titled "Cupid's Nest." The artist is unknown but the paper is watermarked "W. Turner & Son, 1810." These two are typical of a style which was popular before the lace-edged valentine came into vogue.

Plate 90.

The COMET changed to a VALENTINE, for the 14th of February.

Cupid *by the* Comet's *blaze*
Sets Lovers hearts on fire,
Hymen *leads them to the Church*
And makes their bliss entire;
Venus *Goddess of sweet Love,*
In beauty bright does shine,
She with Cupid *makes the Charm,*
To bless each Valentine.

Norcross, New York

Valentine inspired by Halley's Comet in 1835.

116

Plate 91.

Valentine by Kenny
Meadows, dated
1832.

Plate 92.

"Cupid's Nest" by
an unknown artist.

An interesting valentine, which involved careful workmanship, may
be seen in plate 93. It is a double sheet, watermarked "Fellows & Sons,
1821." The conventional border is all handwork in water color, the scroll
being green and the edge of the paper striped in blue. The scene is from
an engraving which has also been hand colored. The author has a pair
of these, both bearing the same watermark. The verse beneath the one
illustrated reads:

> "Oh do kind Cupid aid me pray.
> And make my sweet love kind.
> Great joy and mirth shall crown the day
> That Hymen doth us bind."

The artist for this valentine is not known but the scenes in both have
the appearance of being French.

A number of valentines well known to experienced collectors are
usually referred to as the "Unrequited Love Series." They are aquatints,
in vivid colors, so beautifully executed as to appear like water colors. As
a matter of fact, in this medium, the brightest hues were often added by
hand. The borders in the Unrequited Love Series are always embossed

in the same pattern but the delicately printed, hand-colored design, which surrounds the aquatint, usually varies. The center scenes are apt to border on the dramatic, if indeed they are not devoted to Victorian grief! So far it has been impossible to learn exactly how many were produced in this series but the last count brought the total to seventeen. One of this group is reproduced in plate 94.

An early vogue, for a short time, favoring center medallions in valentines may be noted. Rock & Company, London, are responsible for the charming hand-colored engraving titled "Breaking the Ice" shown in plate 95. The penned verse underneath reads:

> "Dearest in hopes thy heart to gain
> I offer steadfast love for love;
> All other offerings are vain
> If this can insufficient prove."

It is unfortunate that so many of the verses are so inferior to the workmanship on the valentines. However, when they are handwritten, they come from the heart, therefore must be considered as an interesting reflection on the times in which they were composed. This one is marked "Rock & Co." in small letters under the medallion, and the paper has "Rock-London" embossed in a lower corner.

Author's Collection

Plate 94.

Aquatint from a series known as "Unrequited Love."

Rock & Company produced many valentines, among them being some in a large size with a conventional border surrounding an embossed flower (with its Latin name) in natural colors. Another series carries as a decoration, various flowers, skillfully folded to form a puzzle. The hand-painted flower, in natural colors, stands out in high relief, and is surrounded by a border embossed in blue and white.

Dear to the heart of the English is their navy, and it is therefore quite natural we should find many valentines devoted to sailors, sailors' farewells, ships, etc. Still in the medallion style is the particularly attractive one illustrated in plate 96. This is a hand-colored lithograph dating between 1820 and 1830. It is unsigned and does not carry a watermark. The coloring is bright and it represents a choice addition to any collection.

Plate 97 shows another example of the hand-colored lithograph. The gentleman pictured is said to be in the uniform of an officer in the navy, and the valentine dated between 1825-1830. This one is more crudely executed, but any of the naval types are scarce and desirable.

Plate 95.

Early hand-colored lithograph, by Rock & Company, London.

Norcross, New York

120

Now. now. my dear Poll. I'm landed again,
And Shiners great plenty have got.

Let us join Hand & Heart. never to part.
But share for ever our Lot.

Plate 96.

Hand-colored lithograph, "The Sailor's Return," 1820–1830.

121

The Royal Marine, plate 98, was published by W. Evans and is so marked. William Evans, an important draftsman and engraver in London, was one of Bartolozzi's pupils. He engraved portraits of many notable people, including Lord Nelson and Walpole. A great deal of his work is dated around 1810 so "The Royal Marine of 1812" may have been done before 1830, which is the date given this colored lithograph by some experts. It is not known whether or not W. Evans did the original sketch for this valentine. However, it is a popular subject, and it has been reprinted a number of times in articles devoted to valentine lore.

Plate 97.   Hand-colored lithograph of a naval officer, 1825–1830.

A lady waving farewell to her sailor sweetheart was inevitably a popular theme among English valentines. The example shown in plate 99, a colored lithograph, was published by Dean & Company of Threadneedle Street, London. This firm was responsible for a large and varied assortment of valentines, including a number of mechanicals. Some were marked "Sentimental Moveable."

Plate 98. "The Royal Marine," published by W. Evans, c. 1830.

In the group devoted to sailors and related subjects, we must include the ship shown in plate 100. This mechanical, though unmarked, is dated from 1840-1850. The side of the ship opens to reveal a cupid in mid-air, hovering over a sailor who is either reading or writing a letter to his sweetheart. The ship, in full sail, is vividly colored and carries an attractive border design. The verse beneath it reads:

"Oh! True 'tis indeed I would taste of the lip
    That flies from the Cottage, & ventures the Ship,

Your form as fair as ever painter drew,
Your matchless eyes of clear and deepest blue,
The magic smile which lightens up your face
Your silvery tones your thoughts express'd with grace,
Your gentle temper, manners, all combine,
To make me choose thee for my Valentine.

Dean & Co Threadneed[?]

Plate 99.

Hand-colored litho-
graph by Dean &
Company, London.

Norcross, New York

For she who inclines to a sailor's own heart,
In the gale of adversity—never will part.
Let it blow, and blow hard, my own fond one believe,
I will ever be faithful, and never deceive,
In Hymen's own bonds, no intruder should sever,
And living, love on—yes for ever and ever."

The naval subjects must have enjoyed a wide sale in their day but they are scarce items in this country now and consequently are eagerly sought by collectors.

Along about 1840, A. Park, valentine publisher of 47 Leonard Street, London, issued a most amusing series of brightly hued lithographs in which the artist always made a point of placing Cupid in preposterous positions. Plate 101 shows one from this group. Here Cupid is blandly rowing his fair passenger to shore, and in the right direction, for her suitor

Plate 100.

English ship, dating 1840–1850. The side opens to reveal a cupid hovering over a sailor.

I cannot swear, as thousands do.
And witness call the silver moon
To seal the love they never knew.
Then change as lightly and as soon.

Pub by A. PARK 47 Leonard St London

And if at length the hand of fate.
From love and me should far remove thee.
Then, only then, thou'lt know too late.
How much I've lov'd—how much I love thee.

Plate 101.

Hand-colored lithograph, by A. Park, London.
(See also color supplement after page 106.)

126

is standing by. Cupid's quiver of darts hang over a tree branch and the Temple of Love is prominently featured in the background. In other valentines of this series, Cupid is shown emerging from the portrait of a ladylove, perched on a cloud, or standing on a column. A sense of humor is displayed in many other valentines published by Park.

Valentines embellished with a certain type of decoration variously referred to as a "flower cage," a "cobweb," or a "beehive" have been dated by various writers at anywhere from 1814 to 1860. Of course they were made by a number of firms over a period of years, so it is sometimes difficult to do more than approximate their "birth date." A cobweb seems to be a more apt description than any of the others, even though the writer is accustomed to hearing them referred to as "beehives." A cobweb, dated 1848, is pictured in plate 102. It is particularly rare because it carries a double cobweb, and because the border is lithographed with a most attractive design involving cupids and flowers. One of the cobwebs is parted so that the reader may view the attractive face concealed beneath it. The cobweb is usually encountered singly on a double-sheet valentine with an embossed-lace or open-lace edge. It generally, though not always, consists of a central bouquet, etched, hand painted, or lithographed, which has been skillfully cut, so that when a thread or silk or some other device is pulled, the bouquet becomes a cage, through the openings of which is revealed a girl's picture, a cupid, or a scene. Some of the very early examples are entirely decorated by hand.

Plate 103 shows a single cobweb valentine. The cobweb itself is not unusual, but the woodcut border is. One seldom encounters this type today. The edge seems fairly crude and is certainly not as attractive as the embossed or perforated lace border, but it is interesting to own at least one or two of this type. Underneath the cobweb in plate 103 Cupid will be found riding in a chariot and carrying a torch. The card is entitled "The Triumph of Love." Another unusual feature is that the verse beneath the cobweb is upside-down, so one must reverse the valentine in order to read it! There is no indication of the maker, but it dates about 1835.

An example of a beautifully colored lithograph is pictured in plate 104. The little verse inset underneath the sailor reads:

> "Tho absent, still
>   within my heart,
> Thy memory holds
>   its place,
> Too firmly fixed
>   for time or change
> To ever it efface."

First flower of my heart!
Ever dearest!
'Tis not mine to impart,
Though sincerest
Of all the gay crowds that surround thee—
What my bosom has told
To me only:
That thy form I would fold—
Thee—thee only!
And all the blessings of love fling around thee.

Plate 102.

Rare double cobweb with lithographed border, c. 1848.

Plate 103.

Rare cobweb with woodcut border.

This valentine, together with plates 105 and 106, represent an advanced stage in lithography, for the coloring is applied by this method rather than by hand. The elaborate gold border involved a delicate task, however. Specially trained girls blew the gilt powder on the design, which was printed in sizing, and for their skill they received extra pay. This laborious method anticipated our modern-day airbrush work. The coloring in the elaborate floral pattern surrounding the center medallion showing the sailor is particularly pleasing.

The valentine in plate 105 is one of a series of lithographs featuring the same border but with different center medallions. The process of gilding the elaborate scroll design conforms with that of the preceding example. While the formal conventionalized decorative scheme displayed in this series is handsome, it lacks the sentimental appeal of most valentines.

The third valentine in this series, related in style and process of production to those just described, is more interesting than the last, possibly because the design is not so compact (plate 106). Although it gives the impression of having been stenciled, the card was lithographed in yellow, then bronze powder was blown onto it, while the ink was still wet from printing. Except for the colored lithograph of the girl in the center medallion, the finished valentine is all gold and white. It has been related that the girls who were employed for this work at extra wages were given the additional pay to buy milk as a precaution against lung trouble, which might ensue as a result of breathing in so much of the powder-impregnated air. The three valentines produced by similar processes are all thought to date 1860-1870.

Popular at nearly all periods of valentine production were the puzzles, acrostics, and cryptograms. Plate 107 shows an interesting acrostic lithograph which the reader may as well have the pleasure of decipering! The publisher and exact date are unknown.

The mechanical valentine which we have already discussed and seen in other chapters came into vogue about 1840. The embossed (but not perforated) border was first introduced around this time too, but this we see for the first time framing the mechanical in plate 108. The prospective bride and groom are seen strolling about the churchyard and then behold—the door opens and a wedding scene is shown within. So that the view inside could be seen, the door of the church was left open when the photograph was taken. The lithograph is brightly colored and in an excellent state of preservation, which is more than can be said for the border, which has been carelessly handled in years past. Similar church mechanicals were made by Dean & Company, but this one is unmarked.

In the chapter on handmade valentines, those displaying "the knot of love" were introduced. Now in plate 109 we find the lithographed version

130

Plate 104.

Choice lithograph with gold border accomplished by a special process.

131

Norcross, New York

Plate 105.

One from a series having ornate center medallions.

Plate 106.

Interesting design in gold, produced by a special process.

132

Plate 107.

Lithographed
acrostic.

Plate 108.

Lithographed me-
chanical valentine.

Plate 109.

Lithographed "Endless Knot of Love."

134

of the same subject. This example is hand colored, and the lace border is perforated. The gentleman in the scene wears a dark blue coat and his prospective bride is quite dashing in a red coat lavishly trimmed with ermine. He is attempting to interest her in the church nearby. Two pairs of doves suggest that the mating season is not far removed!

The paper in this valentine is watermarked "J. Whatman, Turkey Mill, 1842." It is not long before even the novice collector learns to look for watermarks, and also for the embossed names of publishers, which are so often cleverly concealed in a leaf or detail of the design. A magnifying glass is soon employed in the search, for it is not at all difficult to overlook the marks which mean so much to an experienced collector.

The advent of embossed-lace borders (solid embossing occasionally two inches wide in the earliest examples) was enthusiastically acclaimed. This was followed, rather slowly at first, by the perforated lace, which served as a frame or surrounding for hand-painted centers. The period of embossed and perforated lace extended from approximately 1840 until 1860 and became the golden age of beautiful sentimental valentines.

IX

JOSEPH MANSELL, FANCY STATIONER

1840 — 1850

THE HEYDAY of lace-paper valentines in England occurred between 1840 and 1860. During these years each publisher tried to outdo the other in creating and marketing the most extravagantly beautiful messages from Cupid imaginable. The rivalry became intense, and so *Punch* finally wielded a few whacks at contestants thus: "A modern Valentine Writer says—

> "My rifled breast
> I searched with care,
> And found Eliza lurking there."

To which *Punch* added its barbs, as follows:

"The gentleman's breast must have been very capacious to have allowed Eliza to have remained upon the lurk before the owner of the premises was aware of it. . . . We are compelled to smash the sentiment [of these valentines] even at the risk of bringing a tear into the eye of the milliner's girl or the servant maid, and a snivel into the nose of the too sensitive shop-boy."

Punch really fell short that time for sentiment cannot be smashed, whether it be the Duke of York or the "sensitive shop-boy."

By 1849, exchanging valentines had become so popular that the editor of *Godey's Lady's Book* slyly inserted the following paragraph in an article entitled "New Fashion for Valentines":

"Should a young gentleman wish to express devotion to his lady-love what better mode than to send her on Valentine's Day the Lady's Book. This would cost but $3.00 and every month would bring the moments of his homage."

Every collector of valentines is prone to develop a fondness for the products of one particular English maker. One may believe Kershaw to have produced the most beautiful lace or original ideas, while another

136

Plate 110.

Mansell valentine in cameo embossing, c. 1845.

may argue that Dobbs offers the greatest variety. The decision to devote this chapter solely to Mansell was not made because his valentines are necessarily considered the finest, although they rank as high as any, but rather that through the representative group of his available creations it is possible to reveal the progress in styles as they advanced between 1840 and 1850. We have already observed the change from *handmade* to *hand-decorated* valentines. The next steps were etchings, copperplate engravings, and lithographs. Later, as the country became more sophisticated, embossed and perforated paper lace caught the popular fancy.

The earliest paper lace was apparently developed in England and at first appears to have been copied from the true handmade, or as we are wont to say, "real lace." The first dated valentine carrying paper lace was recorded in Litchfield, England, under date of February 13, 1826. This lace was not perforated and was embossed by hand. Later on, it was pressed by machinery—long before such papers were produced in America. Lace valentines were imported to the United States by various New York firms until Esther Howland began creating them here, still from lace-edged blanks purchased from English makers. George C. Whitney of Worcester, Massachusetts, was one of the first manufacturers to install the necessary machinery for making paper lace in this country.

Joseph Mansell, of 35 Red Lion Square, London, was listed in 1835 as a "Fancy Stationer," and in 1840 was described as "Engraver and Printer." By 1847 he was also a "Wholesaler." Most of the early purveyors of valentines became manufacturers of their own products, including envelopes. If they had a retail shop and sold such items as valentines, they came under the heading of "Fancy Stationer."

One of Mansell's early valentines displays a style of embossing which we know as "cameo." Plate 110 illustrates this type, which appeared in white about 1840. Later, the embossing was elaborately gilded and hand-colored decorations were also added. The one illustrated, dating about 1845, was gilded, the medallion remaining white, with a beautiful hand-colored rose adornment and a verse in dainty Spencerian hand, as follows:

"Thy love unto my heart hath given
The mixed delight of either sphere
All that the spirit seeks in heaven
And all the senses yearn for here."

The handwritten note was still in vogue at this period, and one can only feel that a young girl's heart must have beat a good deal faster when she scanned the penned lines than it did a few years later at the sight of the stereotyped printed verses, which, lacking the personal touch, could be sent to anyone.

Two variations of this valentine are in the author's collection. One

138

Plate 111.

Rare double cobweb
with perforated-lace
border, c. 1845.

Norcross, New York

139

is similar to the illustration in plate 110, except that the figures of the boy and girl are brilliantly hand colored, and the oval medallion has within it an embossed wreath in gold that encircles a piece of red satin on which two sentimental verses are printed in black. The second valentine is all in white and gold, except for the hand-colored figures of the boy and girl. The oval medallion contains a handwritten verse. This probably dated in the early 1840's.

A rare double cobweb with perforated-lace edge is illustrated in plate 111, with the cobwebs opened so that the scenes within may be seen. Beneath the first cobweb are the youth and maiden, with cupids hovering over their heads. The second reveals the bride and groom, with cupids holding a garland over their heads. As stated before, double cobwebs are rare. Even rarer is a valentine with a cobweb in each of its four corners, which is in Mrs. K. Gregory's collection in New York. The process of cutting the difficult cobwebs is known as papyrotamia. It was difficult handwork and increased the cost of these particular valentines considerably. During their vogue, probably every English publisher of valentines presented cobwebs, the usual type being lithographed.

Perhaps the best known Mansell pattern in lace is the one pictured in plate 112. It is one of his most beautiful and must have been one of his most popular, for it was continued over a number of years. The one illustrated is watermarked "Towgood 1850." However, watermarks do not positively date a valentine, as the plates could have been issued say, ten years sooner than indicated.

The center of the valentine paper, in many of the earliest models of this period, was often removed and silk or satin inserted. In this case, an oval medallion of satin was used as a background for a garland of hand painted roses. An embossed silver lyre was pasted in the center and additional flowers laid on. The flowers above and below the medallion were also pasted on, the finer leaves and flowers being painted in with water color. It is interesting to study plates 112 to 116 from the point of view of the lace-pattern background. The same two patterns are used twice with different decorations over them.

Plate 113 carries two smaller valentines, measuring 7 by 4½ inches, both watermarked "Towgood 1851." One can soon learn to date Mansell's valentines, at least approximately, by studying the styles of the various periods which carry authentic date marks. The valentine at the left of this plate has the center removed and a delicate, sheer material inserted, known as aerophane. It was often used, either in white or light pastel shades, for its softening effect on the decoration beneath it. In this instance, the aerophane covers a brightly colored lithograph of an open book, the pages of which display a sentimental message. The book rests against a bouquet of flowers. On the outside of the aerophane is a gold

Plate 112.

Mansell's best-known perforated-lace border.

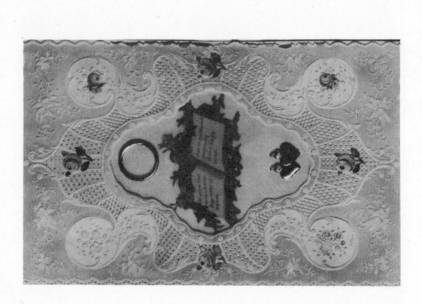

Plate 113. Two Mansell valentines in a smaller size, watermarked "Towgood 1851."

ring of embossed paper, as well as two hearts of the same material. Thus the young lady receives a proposal!

The valentine at the right in plate 113 is not so definite a proposal. The lithographed center has a hand-painted pink rose with green leaves. Above the rose, a brightly colored bird carries a ring in his beak, and below is a motto which reads: "Friendship is like the Suns eternal ray."

Plate 114 illustrates the identical lace pattern used in plate 112, but the design has been gilded, thereby greatly enhancing its beauty. The center is satin with a bouquet of heavily raised flowers, in beautiful shades of color, arranged in the vase by hand. This style dated about 1850. It is of special interest that this particular valentine paper was selected by Their Majesties, King George VI and Queen Elizabeth, to be reproduced for use as a menu for their coronation dinner. The center carried their Royal Arms at the top, and the menu was printed below. Also of interest is the fact that for many years, the musical program to be played at Buckingham Palace concerts was also printed on lace-edged paper, similar to that used for valentines. The author has several in her collection, and one is illustrated in plate 116. These were produced by Ortner & Houle, seal engravers, of 3 St. James Street, S.W.

Embossed envelopes to match the design of the valentine papers were often made and sold to the purchaser. Plate 115 shows one matching the series described. The envelopes were usually the same size as the valentine, thus obviating the necessity of folding, which would mar its beauty.

One of Mansell's most elaborate valentine papers is illustrated in plate 117. As will be noted, the corners and circular border about the medallion are made up of little roses and leaves. The center of this valentine is a sheer material similar to aerophane but has fine pleats through it, so the object beneath is not so clearly seen. In fact, it is almost entirely obscured. In this case, it conceals a lithograph card that has been glued to the second sheet and pictures a young man in a typical Romeo pose, on the doorsteps of his ladylove, who may be seen in a lighted window above him. A cartouche carries the words, "My heart with love is beating." The outside of this valentine has four lithographed wreaths of flowers and in the center, a spray of flowers and wheat, partly in color and partly in gold. This presumably dates about 1845.

Plate 118 illustrates how effective the same lace design as the above becomes when gilded, or in color, or both. In this instance, the roses are in pink and the leaves and conventionalized scrolls in gilt. It would be difficult to imagine a more beautiful valentine! The center is satin, with Cupid standing atop the card bearing the sentimental verse. This valentine is dated 1850 by the Museum of the City of New York, which owns it.

The cameo style of embossing may again be noted in the white val-

Plate 114.

Gilded Mansell, with satin center and built
up bouquet of flowers.

144

Plate 115.

Embossed envelope
to match valentine
paper.

Plate 116.

Perforated-lace-bor-
dered papers were
used for Bucking-
ham Palace musical
programs, dated
1869.

entine shown in plate 119. Some of the beauty is marred, however, by the colored paper that is placed between the first and second sheets so as to bring out the pattern more strongly. This paper is not original to the valentine. The medallion of classical figures, somewhat after the style of Wedgwood, seems slightly out of its element over the mirror edged with frilled lace! Above the medallion, Cupid emerges from the center of a rose—a motif used frequently to decorate valentines of this period.

One could scarcely believe, when first looking at the photographs, that the valentine in plate 120 is the same as the foregoing, with the exception of the coloring and embellishments. Actually, this valentine is nearly all white and gold, though it came to me with silver paper inserted as a background to the design. Silver paper was not needed and actually detracted from its beauty. The center of the valentine is satin, with a gold-paper horn of plenty filled with flowers—beneath the medallion are two embossed lithographs in color, each with a pair of doves in a wreath of flowers. Laid over the center of the valentine is a second tier of lace paper in gold and white with a design of poppies and leaves. In the center of this is an oval medallion of pink aerophane. Once again we see how ef-

Plate 117.

Mansell lace paper employing roses and rose leaves in the border, c. 1845.

Author's Collection

146

Plate 118.

Mansell lace paper with roses and leaves gilded
and hand colored, c. 1850.

147

fective was the use of gilt or bronze, and the manner in which a valentine was decorated. This one is watermarked "Towgood 1854."

A particularly fine pattern of embossed and perforated lace may be seen in plate 121. This valentine is exceptional, in that there are two layers of lace in the center, though these cannot be seen in the picture. A lithographed medallion is covered with a round piece of perforated lace, slightly larger than the medallion. These are in turn covered by the rectangular piece in the strawberry pattern, as may be noted. This top piece is embellished with a bowknot of pink satin ribbon with tiny gold stars attached to it, here and there. The strawberry blossoms, as well as the berries, have been hand colored. The two overlaying pieces of lace

Plate 119. Cameo-style embossing, 1840–1850.

Plate 120. Cameo embossing, heavily gilded.

paper are attached at the top, as "lift-ups" were not being used in England during the 1840's, to which period this valentine belongs. Another Mansell paper lace has the strawberry pattern in the border instead of in the center, as pictured here.

The most elaborate of Mansell's creations is displayed in plate 122. Four layers of fine lace, richly ornamented in gold and silver embossing make it particularly luxurious. The first page has a medallion in blue satin enclosed in a wreath of flowers, with Cupid, two wedding rings, and the word "constant" attached to the satin. The second layer displays a bird-cage effect, revealing two lovers. The third layer carries a white satin center decorated with a ship and flowers, while the fourth has a heart

Plate 121.

Particularly fine perforated lace in an unusual
pattern, partly gilded and hand colored.

150

Plate 122.

One of Mansell's most elaborate creations, consisting of four layers.

151

in the center with a gold harp inscribed, "Reward me with thy love." The fifth page constitutes the back. This is all entirely original and must have been an expensive item, even in the old days.

Every publisher of valentines issued at least some of the fashionable envelope style, or those containing an envelope in which the love message

Plate 123.

Envelope valentine, the message thus being
conveyed privately.

could be enclosed. Mansell was no exception to the rule. Plate 123 illustrates an early one, in which the envelope is a figured silver paper. The wreath below was made by hand; and embossed flowers, silk flowers, and velvet leaves were utilized, together with a vine done in water color. The whole effect is most charming. This valentine dates about 1848.

A Mansell valentine, probably unique in its type of decoration, and titled "A trifle Towards Housekeeping," is shown in plate 124. The en-

Plate 124.

This valentine carries a hint to a prospective
bride, dated 1849.

velope contains, instead of a note, metal knives, forks, and plates, as a gift to the prospective bride! A note underneath says:

"In the first blush of Spring
To my dearest I bring,
The homage that lovers should pay
For the riches of Youth,
Are affection and truth,
The tribute I offer to day."

Beneath the verse is an elaborate wreath, similar to that on the preceding valentine. This valentine is dated 1849.

A design that collectors will learn to identify with Mansell's name is shown in plate 125. It may be all in silver, or in silver with the flowers in color. The one illustrated is in silver and white, with an extra layer in gold and white surrounding the medallion. There are also gold and silver cloth leaves, as well as lithographed flowers in color. It dates approximately 1855. In the writer's collection is the same valentine with colored flowers and leaves in the lace paper. In the center is a large lace-paper

Plate 125.   A Mansell lace paper of the 1850's, in white with silver.

Plate 126.

A mechanical valen-
tine, titled "Such is
Married Life."

Such is married life

Plate 127.

Mechanical valen-
tines became pop-
ular in the 1850's.

envelope with the Temple of Love, a pair of doves, and two cupids worked into the design. Upon unfolding the envelope, one finds a scene in gold filagree, together with a small lithograph of an open book which carries Cupid's message.

Mansell published a number of valentines containing small Baxter prints as a center attraction. After Baxter's patent had been renewed in 1849, notices appeared on the mounts of his prints, stating: "Licenses granted to work the process in Great Britain, 200 Guinea's each." Several firms paid Baxter fifty pounds a year as licensees, among them Joseph Mansell, but unfortunately a valentine displaying a Baxter print is not available for an illustration. The information is given as an incentive for collectors, since the acquisition of one or more would be an interesting and valuable addition to any collection.

Plate 126 illustrates an amusing mechanical of the 1840's by Mansell, titled "Such is married life!" The father is pushing his child in a car-

Norcross, New York

Plate 128.

"Dressed" or "paper-doll" valentine.

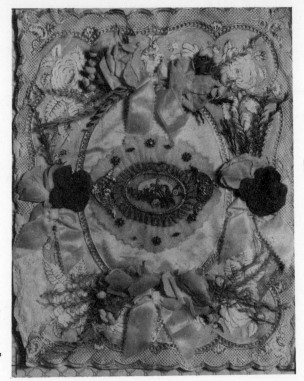

Plate 129.

A Mansell valentine that "choked to death" of its own "too much."

riage, but apparently wishes he were not as he passes a pretty girl! When a tongue of paper (not visible) is pulled, his right arm pushes the carriage.

Another mechanical, still more in the nature of a comic, is shown in plate 127. A paper tongue under the lady's jabot moves her eyes. The scroll carries a short verse, which says:

> "You charm me quite,
> I do not flatter,
> Oblige me pray,
> 'Who is your hatter.'"

A number of mechanical valentines were imported here during the 1840's which did not find favor, and the venture was said to be a loss.

Another type of Mansell, known as the "dressed" or "paper-doll" valentine, found favor during the 1860's. One is shown in plate 128 and an additional example will be found in chapter XI. These consisted for the most part of lithographed faces and feet of boys and girls, the balance of the figure being "dressed." The clothes were fashioned from various sorts of material. The head, collar, hands, boots, and bouquet of the boy in plate 128 are made of paper, while the necktie, trousers, and coat are of cloth. These valentines appeal to doll collectors, as well.

The 1870's witnessed a marked decline in valentine taste. They became decorated with layers of cloth flowers, wax flowers, dried flowers, or seaweed and shells. And so beribboned were they with bowknots of satin that, as one writer expressed it, "They choked to death of their own too much." Plate 129 displays a Mansell along these lines. Though the body of the valentine is from one of his lovely early valentine papers, featuring white roses with gilt, and the center is of satin, what has been done in the way of gaudy embellishments almost defies description!

That the dies and plates for Mansell's lace papers must have been retained for many years is revealed by a recently discovered valentine. The foundation lace is that seen in plate 125. The second layer is Mansell's best-known design and one of his loveliest (plate 112). In the center, in a frame of gold and white embossing resembling Spanish moss, and bedecked all about with applied leaves and flowers, is a bust of Queen Victoria, printed on satin. In this portrait she more nearly resembles the late Queen Marie of Rumania. Printed on the satin below the bust is "Victoria, Queen of England, 1839-1901." Undoubtedly this was a commemorative item in its day, but is of special interest to us now because it reveals that these early valentine papers were reproduced as late as 1901, though for a special purpose.

X

ENGLISH VALENTINE PUBLISHERS

1845 — 1860

AMONG THE EARLIEST English makers of valentines was one H. Dobbs, a favorite of many collectors today because of the wide variety and quality of his output. He apparently began as a paper manufacturer at 8 New Bridge Street, London, in 1803. As nearly as his history can be learned, he took into partnership a man named Pratt, and in 1816 the firm became Dobbs & Company. In 1824 they were listed as "ornamental stationers to the King." Although later on the firm name was changed to Dobbs, Bailey & Company, a London directory as late as 1847 listed the concern as "Dobbs & Co., wholesale, plain and ornamental stationers and pencil makers, 134 Fleet Street & 13 Soho Square." By 1851 Dobbs was in business with William Kidd, who had been established from 1835, as a bookseller and publisher in Hyde Street, Bloomsbury. The business name then became Dobbs, Kidd & Company.

It is thus possible to date Dobbs' work, or at least to approximate the years in which his valentines were produced. His earliest and rarest mark is "Dobbs Patent," printed across one lengthwise end or else underneath the design. Next in order is his "Dobbs" embossed mark, usually found beneath the center decoration. This, as well as "Dobbs & Co.," dates after 1816. Another mark, "H. Dobbs & Co." dates after 1838. "Dobbs, Bailey & Co." apparently first appeared about 1845-1846, and the "Dobbs, Kidd & Co." from about 1851. Collectors find the tracing of dates and identification marks a fascinating pursuit when completing sets produced by the well-known makers of fine valentines.

Plate 130 depicts one of the early, rare Dobbs-Patent creations. Represented is a hand-painted replica of the American ship-of-the-line *Pennsylvania*, a 120-gun warship which was commenced in Philadelphia in 1822 and launched with a complement of 1100 officers and men in 1827. American newspapers must have given the launching considerable publicity for an English valentine maker to reproduce it. Of course Dobbs had in mind the lucrative American market. The *Pennsylvania* was subsequently burned during the Civil War, on order of our government, along with five other ships, to prevent them from falling into the hands

159

Plate 130.

Hand-painted ship *Pennsylvania* bearing
"Dobbs Patent" mark.

of the Rebels. The Dobbs patent refers to the early process of embossing, as displayed in the border of the valentine in plate 130. This one probably dates between 1827 and 1830. In the Norcross collection is a Dobbs-Patent valentine watermarked "Pine Smith & Allnutt—1813."

An interesting early Dobbs valentine titled "Cupid's Pillar Post" pictures an old-time receptacle for letters, with another opening for "answers." Above the mailbox is inscribed by hand, "First read then post this billet doux, And see how love will answer you." This is shown in plate 131.

Valentine manufacturers often continued to use the same patterns in lace paper over a period of years, the only difference being in the type or style of decoration. Thus, it is possible to illustrate two Dobbs creations on the same pattern of lace paper, each displaying a different Dobbs

Norcross, New York

Plate 131.

Dobbs "Pillar Post" valentine mailbox.

mark. The first, in plate 132, is simply marked "Dobbs," so from its general style one would date it from 1840 to 1845. The fruit in the center medallion is made of a fine silk velvet, the leaves of delicate silk, while the vines are painted in water color. The verse above it was penned in color, as was often customary in decorative valentines of this period. Plate 133 shows the same lace-paper pattern. The decoration is closely similar in style, but carries the embossed mark of "Dobbs, Bailey & Co." It will be noted that the floral design under the verse employs some of the same kind of flowers utilized in the preceding valentine. This one must date after Bailey joined the firm, which proves that the same styles endured for some years. There was not the constant demand for change in those days.

A Dobbs, Bailey & Company valentine notable chiefly for penmanship, can be seen in plate 134. Around the top portion is written "A valentine for Miss Anna," and beneath the verse it is dated Brooklyn, February 14, 1845. The envelope was addressed to Miss Anna Gibbs, 93 Henry Street, Brooklyn. The verse is handwritten, and "affection," "love," and "friendship" are stressed. It will again be noted that the lace paper is the same design as on the two preceding valentines. T. W. Strong's "Valentine Depot" in New York sold the imported lace paper with the centers blank, so that a love-lorn youth could make up his own valentine. Embossed envelopes to match could also be purchased.

The same lace-bordered paper sometimes received further elaboration by lace embossing around the center medallion. A particularly handsome valentine of this type by Dobbs, Bailey & Company is shown in plate 135. The center of the medallion is satin and the flowers are embroidered in fine shades of color. The vase, hand-painted on rice paper, was glued in place after the medallion was inserted. Considering its extreme fragility, it is surprising how many valentines of this period used rice paper.[1] In this particular example, the edge of the satin medallion was further enhanced by a narrow border of embossed gold-colored paper, and the sender penned the following lines about the inner border of the valentine:

> "Let soft love beaming from thine eyes
> Speak rapture to my heart
> And like the sun in eastern skies
> Its cheering rays impart."

Plate 136 illustrates a still more elaborately embossed Dobbs, Bailey & Company creation titled "The Barometer of Love." The barometer is labeled "Esteem," "Friendship," "Love," with "Enrapture, Unity & Bliss"

---

[1] A substitute for rice paper was produced from flour and glycerin, which was less subject to breakage, but not so attractive.

Plate 132.

Valentine marked "Dobbs," 1840–1845.

K. Gregory

Plate 133.

Valentine marked "Dobbs, Bailey & Company."

164

Plate 134.

A handwritten
Dobbs, Bailey &
Company valentine,
dated 1845.

Plate 135.

A hand-embroidered
center, on satin,
with rice-paper vase,
Dobbs, Bailey &
Company.

as the highest reading! The embossed flowers in delicate colors are the early type, set up and pasted on by hand. This most unusual and choice valentine dates around 1845.

The valentines shown thus far are a good indication of the high quality of Dobbs' work, both before and after he formed a partnership with

K. Gregory

Plate 136.

"The Barometer of Love," by Dobbs, Bailey & Company.

Bailey. The next few examples are taken from the time he was associated with William Kidd, and would therefore date from about 1851.

Every so often something new in decorative schemes for valentines appeared, and the Dobbs, Kidd & Company idea of utilizing spun glass in color was an innovation. Plate 137 displays the use of this material most effectively. The center figure in the medallion, "A Pet Dove," is mounted on aerophane, which is in turn attached to some very fine net.

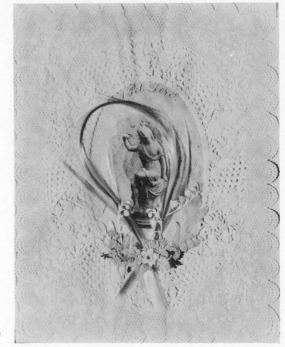

Plate 137.

Spun glass utilized to decorate this valentine by Dobbs, Kidd & Company.

Norcross, New York

The beautifully designed embossed- and perforated-lace paper is apparently of the 1850's.

Several of the early manufacturers issued valentines with birds as the principal attraction, but none are quite so appealing as the series put out by Dobbs, Kidd & Company. Plate 138 displays two that would date in the 1850's. In most cases, lithographed birds are mounted on hand-painted backgrounds, the card sometimes being further embellished by the addition of applied leaves, flowers, or even dried grasses. The chicken at the left of plate 138 is an especially realistic-looking bird and over her is inscribed "For my dear chick with love sincere." The second valentine is called "Rural Lovers." The nest is placed among some cherry blossoms and dried grasses are added to the background. Plate 139 displays the next in the series, entitled "Love Birds." This is one of the finest in the group, the lace paper being so realistic as to appear like genuine lace. The center medallion is surrounded with a gilded wreath of flowers, and the page in the open book below the birds reads:

> "More closely bound than friend or brother,
> One cannot live without the other."

167

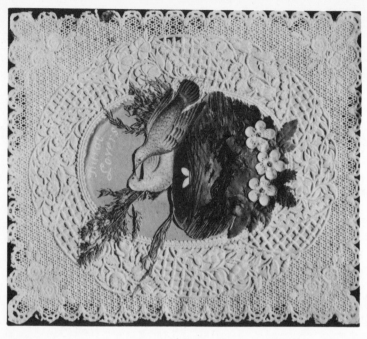

Norcross, New York

Plate 138.

A chicken and birds decorate two valentines by Dobbs, Kidd & Company.

Plate 139.

Unusually delicate
lace and a pair of
love birds combine
in a charming valen-
tine by Dobbs, Kidd
& Company.

Norcross, New York

Plate 140.

Two busy birds en-
gaged in building a
nest, enhance this
valentine.

169

Norcross, New York

Plate 141.

A frog is applied against a hand-painted background in this unusual paper-lace valentine.

Two birds engaged in building a nest is the subject of the fourth valentine, shown in plate 140. The lace paper is in an entirely different pattern, slightly more rococo in effect, and the background of the medallion is cloth. The roof of the house is a colored lithograph and the birds, flowers, and foliage are also applied. Considerable handwork is apparent in these early valentines—time-consuming work that would make them extremely costly to assemble, thinking in terms of present-day labor costs.

The last in this particular series by Dobbs, Kidd & Company, deviates from the others by utilizing a frog as the center attraction. The background of plate 141 is hand painted, and Mr. Frog and the little polliwogs are applied. A little humor is injected in the lines penned about the center, which say:

"Why! You don't mean to say 'you'll not marry me.' What next? As the Frog said when his tail fell off."

This group would make a most interesting addition to any collection.

One more Dobbs-Kidd valentine, probably dating in the early 1860's, is shown in plate 142. The background lace is white, with silver and white lace superimposed. The chromo-lithograph in the center is surrounded by a medallion in gold paper lace. The front is held up by use of small folders of stiff paper. At this period it will be noted that English valentines occasionally make use of folders between the layers of lace,

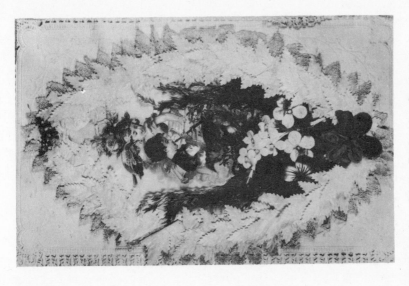

Plate 142.   Left: Dobbs, Kidd & Company valentine of the 1860's.   *Right:* A valentine by Mullord, decorated with a wreath of cloth leaves.

which cause the second or top tier to remain extended from the basic layer. This innovation, apparently started by Esther Howland, gained in popularity in this country but was not featured by the English.

A creator of lovely valentines whose name is not frequently seen in this country was Joseph Addenbrooke. Little is known about him except that he was among the early makers, as evidenced by specimens of his work. Plate 143 exhibits an excellent example. The center of the medallion is satin, with a cupid in gold holding a classical style bust of a girl suspended from a painted ribbon. The flowers are embossed in color and have been painstakingly glued in place by hand. It has "Love to valentine" written in small, fine script. This is a choice valentine of the highest standard.

There are apparently few records in regard to Addenbrooke in this country. However, he is listed in an 1841 London directory as "Joseph Addenbrooke & Co., fancy stationer, 101 Hatton Garden." A few years later his name appears simply as "Joseph Addenbrooke, manufacturer of ornamental stationery and envelopes, Bartlett's Building."

Plate 144 shows a particularly delicate and lovely double lace-paper Addenbrooke, opened so that the full effect may be seen. The two sheets of lace paper were made in one and simply folded in the center. When the valentine is closed, the rose on the second sheet shows through the open filigree of lace on the first. This example appears to be of the late 1850's or early 1860's, as it has two tiers of lace on the face, the second tier supported by paper folders. It is unfortunate that more cannot be learned about Addenbrooke and his work at this time.

Another producer of valentines, who must have entered the field at an early date, is T. H. Burke of 12 Bull Head Court, Newgate. Plate 145 presents one which might very well date prior to 1840. The embossed edge is solid, not perforated, and the center contains a hand-colored lithograph which has been pasted in. The design surrounding the medallion is printed lightly in gold. The flowers are hand colored and glued in place, the smaller leaves being painted in water color directly on the card. Burke's name is embossed in small letters, in the lower right-hand corner.

A second Burke, which also appears to date around 1840, may be seen in plate 146. This one employs the same lace edge, semi-perforated, but with the addition of a heart-shaped medallion of lace, the attractive flowers in the center being entirely hand painted. Burke's lace border, with the bird surmounting the column on each side, is distinctive and, as in the case of Addenbrooke, causes one to wish more might be learned about him and his work. In the author's collection is a smaller Burke valentine, measuring 5¾ by 4 inches. This has an attractive perforated-lace edge and a center decoration of hand-painted flowers in water color.

Plate 143.

Paper-lace valentine by Joseph Addenbrooke.

173

Plate 144.   Unusually delicate double paper-lace valentine by Addenbrooke.

Combined with brightly colored silk leaves and flowers, the total effect is charmingly quaint and old fashioned.

Delarue & Company is a name familiar to most collectors of old valentines. In an English directory the name is spelled De La Rue, but it appears written either way on his valentines. This firm of card makers, embossers, and fancy stationers was established at 20 Finsbury Place, London, in 1835. Their products are not encountered in this country as frequently as are those by Mansell, Kershaw, Dobbs, and other well-known names of this period, so their production was probably not as prodigious. The handsome Delarue valentine in plate 147 is embossed in the heavier cameo style. Mounted on a satin background, a delicately colored embossed cupid kneels in a bower, his hands clasped in prayer, while a dove wings a message to the loved one. It is an altogether charming valentine, measuring 7½ by 6 inches. A Delarue in the author's collection, slightly smaller, is embossed solidly in a rose-trellis design, with a conventional edge formed of single rose leaves. Two kneeling figures surmount a center medallion which holds a basket of flowers, marked "Forget-Me-Not." Inside is penned the following verse:

"Susie, how I love that name—
It can never breathe of shame—
Gentle as the heart that bears it
Blest the youth who takes and shares it!
A new valentine of roses
In her cheek each spring discloses
To the eye of every swain.
But alas, they sigh in vain.

Plate 145. An early embossed-lace valentine, with hand-colored lithographed center, by Burke, c. 1840.

Yet most lovely Susie dare I
Hope that we are doomed to marry?
If so it is, you'll find me true,
Girl of my heart's love, gentle Sue!"

This homemade proposal in verse, unsigned, was discovered in a lovely embossed envelope, unaddressed! Let us hope Susie's suitor was not too shy to send it!

David Mossman of Islington (1825-1901) produced some beautiful valentines, though his name is not quite as well known as several of his contemporaries. The valentine in plate 148, with its lyre of gold em-

Plate 146. Dignity of paper lace design is displayed in this Burke.

Author's Collection

Plate 147.   An unusually charming creation by Delarue &
Company of London.

bellished with eagles' heads, all mounted on delicate gauze, is one of his
unusual creations. It is difficult to decide whether this valentine is more
beautiful with the lyre gilded or left white, for it may be found both
ways. Plate 149 (left) displays another enchanting example of Mossman's
work. Smaller in size, this one appears to date about 1840. Part of the
flowers in the center medallion are hand colored and applied, the balance
being filled in with water color. Mossman's workmanship is distinctive
and any of his valentines enhance a collection. The example at the right
is of the same period but is unsigned.

Records in this country do not reveal just how early George Kershaw
was making valentines, but judging solely by specimens of his work, it

must have been not much later than 1840. His name appears in a London directory of 1851 as "George Kershaw & Son, wholesale stationers, envelope and steel pen manufacturers, 17 Wilderness Row." Most of his valentines bear an embossed "Kershaw," while others appear as "Kershaw & Son" or simply "G. Kershaw."

Plate 150 illustrates an attractive valentine marked "Kershaw & Son." This is another example showing the heavy cameo type of embossing. Against the silk background a child kneels with arms outstretched to his little love. In the author's collection is a similar valentine depicting the same scene, and with it is the original embossed envelope. Curiously, the envelope has embossed under the flap "N.Y. Val. Co."—meaning "New York Valentine Co." Since Kershaw was a manufacturer of envelopes, these must have been made to order for the concern in New York.

The smaller valentine in plate 150, with the same cameo style of embossed paper, is also marked "Kershaw & Son." Woven in the design at the upper edge are the words, "True Love." Collectors should not underestimate the charm of the small valentines, which have a great deal of appeal. Moreover, many of them are rarer than some of the large ones.

Plate 148.

An interesting design by David Mossman.

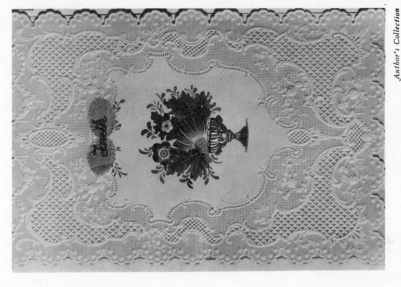

Plate 149. Two choice valentines of the 1840's, displaying early method of decorating center medallions. The one at the left is by Mossman, the one at the right is unsigned.

179

Plate 150.

Cameo-type embossing **is** displayed in these
two valentines by Kershaw & Son.

The reason that comparatively few small valentines are illustrated here is
that they tend not to show all the details as well.

Plate 151 displays a charming design in lace paper, as well as a most
attractive hand-colored lithograph. The lady has received her message
from Cupid and is now being blindfolded by her suitor. A brief verse is
penned above the lithograph. This valentine, simply marked "Kershaw,"
probably dates in the early 1840's.

A dainty "envelope" valentine by Kershaw appears in plate 152. The wreath encircling the envelope is lithographed and colored by hand. The verse penned above and below the envelope reads:

> "Though absent still within my heart
> Thy memory holds its place
> Too firmly fixed for time or change
> To ever it efface."

The note in the center is dated "184–" indicating that this item was carried from year to year during the 1840's.

An interesting variation of the "envelope" valentine—also by Kershaw—is shown in the example at the left of plate 153. It is decorated by hand in water color, and the small envelope attached to the center unfolds, revealing a space for a very private little note inside. This valentine, along with some thirty-five others produced by various makers, came to me from a friend who collected them in England while living there some years ago. All with the exception of the lithographs, are handmade on lace-bordered paper and many carry a handwritten message. One might expect the sender *always* wrote the sentimental lines but such is not the case. The fact that all the valentines in this group were unused proves that the stationery stores sold many cards with the messages penned in ink, ready for mailing. Besides these and the decorated valentines with blank spaces left open for those who preferred to write their own verses, still other cards were "blanks" or lace-bordered valentines devoid of any decoration for the industrious youth who wanted to decorate his own as well as pen an endearing message.

George Kershaw was undoubtedly among the most prolific of the valentine makers of his time and is therefore a favorite of many collectors. In the author's collection are a number of his creations, all in their original envelopes and addressed to two sisters who lived in Cambridgeport, Massachusetts. Some of the envelopes are of beautiful embossed lace, matching the lace paper of the valentine. One of the valentines is all white, entirely made up of the finest in perforated lace. It has a heart in the center, embossed with these words: "Wanted a Sweet." It was posted as late as February 18, and five cents carrying charge was paid on it. Many valentines, in the old days, were posted either before or after Valentine's Day.

Windsor is another name familiar to all collectors of Cupid's messages. John Windsor was in business in 1840, at which time he was described as a "cardmaker" of Vineyard Walk, Clerkenwell. In 1844 he was listed as a "Book and print seller" and in 1847 as an "enameled card manufacturer, 2 Meredith Street, Clerkenwell." In 1851 he was engaged as "card maker and manufacturer of fancy boxes at 23, Coppice Row, Clerkenwell." The "fancy boxes" may very well indicate the popular

K. *Gregory*

Plate 151.

Choice hand-colored lithograph with embossed-lace border, by Kershaw.

Plate 152.

A choice envelope valentine, surrounded by
hand-painted wreath, by Kershaw.

183

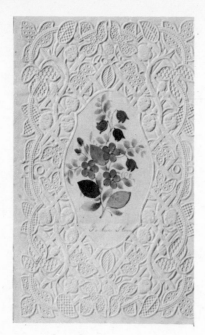

Plate 153.

Above: An early embossed paper by Meek.

Right: Kershaw, with hand-painted envelope center.

ornamental boxes made to hold the shadow-box valentines. Plates 48, 74, and 75 illustrate three of these.

Two valentines by Windsor are shown in plate 154. The lady with the lace skirt may be seen in several of Windsor's creations. She appears in various poses, but always in the same type of gown. The background under the white lace front is always in color, often green or blue. In this case, it happens to be red, resembling a watered silk. Cupids are generally in evidence, often above or below the design.

The second valentine in plate 154 is white, lavishly decorated in gold. The lace curtain has a blue ribbon attached to it, by which it may be lifted to reveal a separate scene, featuring an embossed cupid against a

Plate 154. Two valentines by Windsor, of the 1850's.

185

background of white silk. Both sheets of this valentine are of lace paper, which not only carry Windsor's name, but also a British registry mark.

The Windsor at the top of plate 155, made in the 1850's, is decorated with colored wafers of paper, such as were described in the chapter on Esther Howland. The one behind the figure at the left is orange, the one at the right is magenta, and the one forming the background to the group of cupids is green. This valentine is typical of the 1850's.

The valentine at the lower left of plate 155 carries an embossed bust of Queen Victoria as a young woman. This would seem to date the valentine between 1848-1850. The background is orange, with a vivid blue behind the reclining figures.

Windsor's name is cleverly hidden beneath the feet of one of the cupids in the sweet little valentine at the lower right of plate 155. The cupid in the medallion is a chromo-lithograph, mounted on a fine net. The most amusing part of this cameo embossed-lace valentine is the mute message it imparts! Sewed to the inside of the back page is the tiniest of hand-knitted mittens! It measures a scant three-quarters of an inch in length. Perhaps all readers are not familiar with the old-time expression, about a girl giving her beau "the mitten." In modern slang, a youth is "given the gate." So unhappy the boy who received this valentine, along with "the mitten"!

An unusually attractive example of a Windsor of a later date is shown in plate 156.

Not much is known about George Meek of Crane Court, Fleet Street, except that we find his valentines here rather frequently. He produced, among his varied assortment, an attractive series of mechanical flowers which, when opened by means of a cardboard tongue, reveal the head of a maid or youth. One may be seen in plate 157. A complete set of these flowers offers the pleasure of the chase to any collector who essays to assemble them.

Plate 153 displays a typical Meek valentine. The paper, once more, is embossed cameo style, and the center medallion has a few hand-colored paper flowers stuck on with background leaves painted directly on the sheet in water color. Underneath is written, "To her I love." Plate 158 shows another of Meek's patterns in solid embossing. The flowers in the center are also embossed and colored by hand.

While many Meek valentines display a tendency toward solid embossing, he produced all types. The valentine at the right in plate 158 represents a style that was popular in the late 1860's—when the lush days of the Victorian era were being felt. It is all gold and white against a bright blue background. The figures in the center, as well as the other two ornaments, are German chromo-lithographs. It is an attractive valentine of its period, which reflects changing moods in styles.

Three valentines by Windsor, of the 1850's.

Plate 155.

Three of Meek's valentines of the late 1850's, together with one of his embossed envelopes, are shown in plate 159. They are all white lace, lavishly gilded and with colored backgrounds in which varying shades of red are prominent. The three valentines are typical of the early days of Esther Howland, and they are decorated much in the manner that she would have done them.

What Meek & Son were doing with valentines in the Gay Nineties may be seen in plate 160. This gaudy affair, typifying the general trend, consists of three layers. The base is a heavy double sheet, embossed and printed with much gold and color. The second layer is silver lace and forms a background for the central figure that, mounted on narrow folders, is thus raised from the base. The third layer is of coarser silver lace, embellished with a number of cupids, butterflies, and flowers, which extends out so that it forms a frame for the figure. Whether the lady is some famous actress of her day or merely a fanciful figure is not known

Plate 156.

A Windsor of the late 1860's.

188

Plate 157.

A mechanical valen-
tine by Meek.

Plate 158.

Two valentines by Meek:
right: in early 1840's;
left: in late 1860's.

at present. The inside of the folder carries a verse which reads as follows:

"It is the summer of my life,
Yet I grow older every year;
It's time, I think, to take a wife
Without delay. What think you, dear?"

So the proposals still went on, via Cupid's messages.

A London directory of 1847 lists G. Ingram of City Road—a name familiar to collectors of valentines. Many of his creations simply bear an embossed "Ingram" while others have "Ingram London" and still others carry his street address, along with his name. Two examples of his work may be seen in plate 161.

Rimmel was another name to be conjured with in the valentine world of old London, for it was he who introduced the valentine sachet. One may be seen at the right of plate 162, all done up in purple with a bouquet of violets adorning it. It was heavily padded, and doubtless heavily scented, too, though the fragrance has long since departed. Rimmel's offerings along this line finally developed into such elaborate and costly items that they were said to have sounded the death knell of the less expensive valentines for a time. However, Rimmel's valentines were not devoted entirely to sachets. Plate 162 also displays one of his dainty lace creations, which is all white and gold. A colored lithograph in the center depicts Cupid holding a basket of flowers on his head. Rimmel produced a number along this same line. They carry an embossed message at the top, such as "Love's Visions," while in the lower border an embossed cartouche marked "E. Rimmel, perfumer, London" is usually found. Two additional creations by Rimmel are to be seen in plate 163.

Another English valentine maker whose name is familiar to collectors though little is known about him is Mullord. Plate 142 displays an interesting example of his work, which probably dates about 1859-1860. Mounted on embossed paper with a narrow lace edge is a wreath of leaves in a fine white cloth, laid against a backing of delicate lace. The background of the medallion is a firm white material. Below the chromolithograph of the little boy and girl are several very realistic flowers, in silk velvet. Dried grasses and seaweed in green and brown also figure in the decorative scheme. Altogether, it is quite an interesting valentine, reflecting as it does a transitional period in valentine styles. It is simply marked with an embossed "Mullord."

Two other valentines by this maker, both identified by a "Mullord Bros." mark, are shown in the upper row of plate 164. One is an attractive cameo-embossed lace in which doves are the principal motif. The other displays the embossed lithograph background for paper lace, which marks the beginning of the end for really fine valentines. This later speci-

Plate 159.

Three valentines by Meek and an embossed
envelope.

Plate 160.

A Meek & Son valentine of the Gay Nineties.

192

Right: The smallest
lace valentine in
the author's collec-
tion (actual size).

Two valentines by
Ingram.

Plate 161.

Author's Collection

193

men is of the 1870's. Two more examples in paper lace by "Mullord," which appear to date in the 1860's, are shown in plate 165.

An attractive small valentine by a little-known maker is shown at the lower left of plate 164. Along the folded border is embossed, very lightly, "Bollans." Perhaps more light will be shed on him and his work in the future. As stated before, the little valentines, that is, those measuring 3½ by 2½ inches up to 3¾ by 2¾ inches, offer considerable in the way of interest and charm, and should not be overlooked. The smallest valentine in the author's collection (plate 161) measures 2¾ by 1¾ inches. It is of delicate lace and appears to date about 1845-1850.

Plate 166 displays three valentines marked "Wood." An English writer mentions an S. T. Wood of 268 Strand, whose name appears on some rather sketchily drawn comics. The author has been unable to find his name in English directories of 1847 and 1851 but did find a Thomas Wood, listed as a "wholesale stationer, engraver, and printer of 24 Milk Street, and Godfrey's Court." It would seem reasonable to believe that those illustrated might be from this latter source, since they are of the 1840-1850 period. These few examples were available to illustrate but may not be representative of his finest creations. Both Esther Howland and

Plate 162. Two valentines by Rimmel, the one on the right with a heavily padded sachet.

MY LIFE HAS BEEN ONE THOUGHT OF LOVE

194

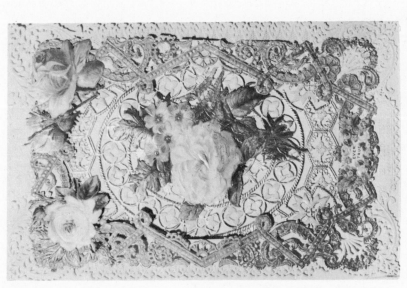

Plate 163.   Two attractive Rimmel valentines in white and silver, with roses in color.

George C. Whitney bought lace paper from Wood and this connection may be the reason why many smaller valentines bearing his imprint are found in this locality.

The largest valentine in plate 166 has an embossed border and a delicate lace center. Under the top layer is a smaller valentine, attached to the second page, the outer edge of which is striped in red.

The second largest valentine in plate 166 is embossed and gilded. The center medallion is of net and lifts up to reveal a book containing a verse titled "Love." The background is a deep magenta, which is the reason the valentine appears so dark in the photograph. The smallest of these three valentines is embossed in white, with a bright blue background which shows through the lace. Wood contrived to mark his work in such a way that it is not always easy to find. The largest valentine has his name embossed on the lengthwise fold, but the next in size has "Wood" in diminutive letters on the bottom rail of the fence, while the smallest valentine has his name at the base of the white medallion.

Elaborate valentines created by Wood in the 1870's—two-, and three-tiered affairs built up to fit into fancy ornamental boxes—have considerable appeal, for they were not all in poor taste, by any manner of means. They bring back nostalgic memories of a happier, peaceful world to those who may still remember when they were in vogue in this country during the 1880's.

All collectors of valentines are familiar with the name of Jonathan King of London, who was not only a manufacturer but the greatest amasser of Cupid's messages in the world. He collected full sets of valentines by the various makers, year in and year out, until his accumulation, in actual weight, amounted to about eight tons. Many were doubtless from his own manufactory and of a late period. The collection was offered to the British Museum but they did not have the space to house it properly. A number, however, were accepted by the London Museum, and the bulk of the rest of the collection was stored in a warehouse. Tragedy struck when the warehouse caught fire in 1918, and a large portion of the contents was consumed in flames. Fortunately, all the vast collection was not in storage. Many of the King valentines and scrapbooks found their way into the hands of London dealers, and as a result many fine specimens have been slowly seeping into this country.

A few other English makers of note, examples of whose work do not happen to be illustrated, include: H. A. Sanders of 7 Red Lion Court and Fleet Street, who was in business during the 1840's-1850's and produced some very fine perforated-lace paper; A. Cortman, known to be making valentines in the late 1840's; John Evans of 26 Budge Row, Cannon Street; J. Murray, who produced early lithographed borders with the center designs colored by hand; J. L. Marks, maker of various types, in-

Right and below:
Two valentines by
Mullord.

Below: A small Bollans.

Above: A small Mansell.

Plate 164.

cluding comics, also a series with fine borders lithographed in black on pastel-colored backgrounds; Kendrew, of York, who was responsible for some early uncolored valentines, classical style, printed from copperplates; E. Lloyd of Broad Street, Bloomsbury, whose firm was established in 1800; Westwood, who did some charming "cobwebs"; R. Carr, of

Plate 165. Two valentines by Mullord.

Houndsditch; G. Gilbert; Pickering & Co.; J. Robey & Sons, Leamington, manufacturers of valentines about 1859-1869; Elliot, of Holywell Street, who introduced a series in which ladies appeared composed of flowers, fruit, or vegetables; Robert Canton of 7 Dowgate Hill and 172 Aldersgate Street, London, who issued a twelve-page catalogue, December 10, 1863, describing his superior valentines of every variety, and J. Harwood of 26 Fenchurch Street. Other recognized names are Goode Brothers; K. Sutton; J. Robinson of Glasgow, who printed some early classical engravings designed by Keech; and Bartholomew F. Lloyd & Company, of Edinburgh, who had an office at 29 Thavies in London, and at 44 Hanover Street, Edinburgh. Mr. Lloyd was said to be one of the most famous lithographers in Scotland from the 1840's.

The valentine business involved more than meets the eye. A tremendous amount of material of various sorts entered into their production. During one year, about 1851, it is claimed that an English firm spent

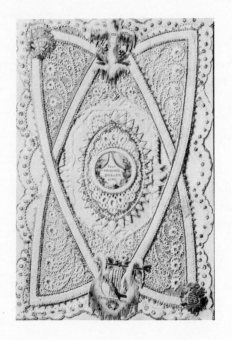

Plate 166.

Three valentines by
Wood.

nearly $5,000 a week for artificial flowers, solely for the purpose of ornamenting valentines. Satin was purchased in five-thousand-yard lots. Paper lace ran about $17,000 per year, while the boxes in which they were sent cost nearly $5,000 more. Additional decorations which found favor at this period, in the way of bird of paradise feathers, humming birds, and perfume for the sachet valentines, ran into a small fortune. As time went on and valentines became more and more elaborate, the expense involved for silk, lace, velvet, net, spun glass, plush, and looking glasses was almost fantastic. Less expensive materials were finally utilized, such as dried flowers, seaweeds, shells, and ornaments made from cork.

Aside from the quantity of exports England shipped to this country during the 1840's and 1850's, she received a considerable source of revenue from valentines sent to her colonies, particularly during the time of the Australian Ballarat gold rush. The London stationers received requests for a special line of valentines at this time, which could not be too elaborate to suit the gold miners. As a result, a special valentine two feet long was created, which it is said was outlined in gold and silver lace, with beautifully painted panels. Everything imaginable in the way of bright objects to attract the eye were used as decoration, such as silk, lace, fruit, flowers, feathers, and imitation jewelry. Others followed, similarly gaudy, and they cost the customers anywhere from ten to twenty-five pounds (approximately $50 to $250)—or a bag of gold! But even these did not entirely suit. The next order requested that more gold be used. It would be interesting to own one of these elaborate concoctions but so far as is known, none ever reached this country.

XI

ENGLISH VALENTINES, UNMARKED

IN COLLECTING VALENTINES, one will find many highly desirable, as well as rare examples, which do not bear any maker's stamp. While it is often possible to identify a specimen by the border pattern, there are still bound to be a certain number of fine valentines in every collection which may remain unnamed as to publisher. This chapter is devoted to those rarities.

Of interest is the hand-colored lithograph in plate 167, with its attractive embossed border. The gentleman is gazing into Hymen Jewelry store, with signs reading "Wedding rings. No goods exchanged" and "Chains warranted to wear well." The verses read:

> "You promised me on Monday last,
> A present you would bring;
> Or take me out a pleasant walk,
> To buy some pretty thing.
>
> Tomorrow I shall be at home,
> Of love, a token bring;
> And when you come with rat-tat-tat,
> Pray don't forget the ring."

Thus we see how the gold digger of the 1850's operated!

The valentine in plate 168 is an early hand-colored engraving, with a handsomely embossed design in the border. The lady is being led toward the distant church, though it appears she is having to be persuaded! There is no personal message, nor even a watermark to be found on this specimen.

Many might consider the remarkable valentine in plate 169 to be one of the finest illustrated in this volume, if not the very best. The embossed paper represents a remarkable piece of work. The small medallion is satin and mounted in the center is the Temple of Love in mother-of-pearl. Curiously, the small inscription beneath it is in German, the translation reading "May this be a symbol to you." While many of the brilliantly embossed ornaments for use in decorating valentines were made in Ger-

Plate 167.

Hymen Jewelry
Store.

many, the Germans as a people are not associated with the production of valentines, nor of celebrating St. Valentine's Day in anything like the same manner as the English and Americans. Many other countries, however, have observed the day by the sending of tokens, and even the Chinese had their valentines! The French produced a certain number, too, though the cards did not sell well in America. The observance of St. Valentine's Day has been, and in all probability always will be, largely Anglo-Saxon in character.

One of the most charming valentines in the author's collection is the one shown in plate 170. It consists of a single sheet of very thin paper edged with delicate, fragile perforated lace. An aquatint graces the center medallion, and on either side are delicate flowers, hand colored, with the vines in the background added in water color. It may date as early as 1835.

Four examples of charming small valentines, all hand decorated, may be seen in plate 171. The one at the upper left has a great deal of appeal. The little hummingbird resting at the edge of her nest is beautifully executed in water color. Inside is a personal note "For James" and it is dated 1846. The one next to it in the upper row is edged in blue,

Plate 168.

Early embossed val-
entine, c. 1840.

Author's Collection

American Antiquarian Society

Plate 169.

An extraordinarily
beautiful embossed-
lace valentine, with
Temple of Love in
mother-of-pearl on
satin background.

Plate 170.   Early single-sheet valentine, decorated by hand, c. 1838.

with a hand-painted rose in the center, while the valentine at the lower left is quite similar, apparently produced by the same maker. The valentine at the right, however, has a colored embossed border, which is unusual, and the leaves and tulip in the center have been applied. As is so often the case during this period, the finer, smaller leaves are hand painted. These examples contribute further evidence that small valentines should have a place in every collection. Those devoted solely to the large, elaborate examples can border on the monotonous.

The favorite cobweb valentine in the author's collection is illustrated in plate 172. The double sheet of paper is very thin, and the perforated-paper-lace edge is so delicate as to be almost fragile. The flowers in the center are brilliantly hand colored. When the cobweb is lifted by a thread attached to the center, a garland of flowers is seen surmounted by a blazing heart, pierced with an arrow. Inscribed underneath this is: "Faithful to the last." The verse reads:

"Oh! Flowers, my love, are sweetest
In the Spring time of the year,
And my willing heart, may well impart,
A Lay to one so dear.

Plate 171.

Four small valentines, of an early date, with hand-painted centers.

In Summer's showers—or April's flowers,
My heart would still incline, love,
To join with thee in Love's own bowers,
A happy valentine, love."

Although this valentine has considerable appeal, there are undoubtedly finer ones embellished with cobwebs. In fact, plate 173 reveals a particularly handsome one, the paper lace being beautifully gilded. The open cobweb reveals a rather grown-up cupid, about to lose his bow and arrow to a pretty young miss. This one is watermarked 1856.

No collection is complete without at least one example of the brilliantly illuminated lettering, so popular during the era of perforated lace. Plate 174 illustrates a particularly interesting specimen, the center mounted on a very fine net. It is a song, the first letter of each line spelling out the name of Caroline. It reads thus:

"Come dwell with me, come dwell with me
And our home shall be the humble cot,
Rejoicing where that home may be
On fertile hill, love's hallow'd spot
Love shuns the price of gay saloon
It flies away from there too soon.
Nor stays in where deceit beguiles,
Endangered by corruption's smiles."

The valentine in plate 175 is watermarked "Venables & Co. 1846." Venables was a papermaker who was listed in London directories during the 1840's and 1850's. He may have been in business earlier—and later. The valentine is interesting because this particular lace border may be encountered in color. The one illustrated has a border in light green lace, while the lace medallion in the center is gilded. The cloth flowers with gold leaves are mounted on aerophane of a soft cream color. In the author's collection is another example in the same lace pattern, which is blue with an all-white center. The flowers are applied, and there is a verse above and below the medallion. This valentine was never presented to anyone, indicating once more that verses were sometimes penned in for the benefit of those who did not wish to write their own. A third example of this identical valentine has a rose-pink lace edge. The center is again white with a blue morning glory and green leaves applied. A running line of verse is penned around the four sides. All three valentines bear the 1847 watermark.

The wreath of flowers decorating the valentine in plate 176 is the most unusual I have encountered. It represents a tremendous amount of work, as each flower and leaf is set up by hand. Moreover, mounting

Oh! Flowers, my love, are sweetest
In the Spring time of the year;
And my willing heart may well impart,
A lay to me so dear.

In Summer's showers — or April's flowers,
My heart would still incline, love;
To join with thee in Love's own bowers,
A happy Valentine, love.

Author's Collection

Plate 172.

Unusually fine cobweb with embossed-lace
border.

K. Gregory

Plate 173.

Cobweb on particularly handsome gilded lace
paper.

208

these on the paper so they would remain intact over the years demanded additional patience and skill. These floral motifs were first hand-punched with dies, then colored in. Before the hand-punching process was introduced, the shaping, rounding, and hollowing, as well as the painting of decorative motifs, were all handwork, the fine thin designs in the earliest valentines being very dainty. Later on, such motifs were embossed by use of dies, then sandpapered off at the back. The early dies were made of thick steel. Certain of the flowers were punched out on a sheet of lead, and then colored by hand. Still later, flowers and borders were embossed

Plate 174.   Illuminated lettering on fine net background.

Plate 175.

Paper lace in two colors feature this valentine.

under heat with a tool. After this, came the German "swags" or "scrap," which were sold in sheets (plate 177).

An interesting example of embossed paper, part of which has been gilded, may be seen in the valentine with its original envelope shown in plate 178. The valentine has a larger satin center than is usually encountered, and this is embellished with a bird, the Temple of Love, Cupid's darts, love birds, a heart, two little lambs, and last but not least, the wedding ring!

Two very different valentines are pictured in plate 179. The upper one carries a verse which asks:

"Can Hearts in which true love is plighted,
By weal or woe be disunited?
No! They the storms of life defy,
So let the hearts of
U & I."

The second valentine displays a good bit of ingenuity and at the same time a note of humor has been injected. It is titled "The United Serv-

Plate 176.

Unusual wreath of embossed flowers, set up and applied by hand.

Plate 177.

Author's Collection

Colored ornaments to decorate valentines came
in sheets and were then cut apart.

212

ice." Each piece of the service is depicted as having been broken and then riveted together. Below the dishes a wedding ring is inscribed: "Just one rivet more." This valentine is unquestionably by Dobbs but since it is unmarked, it has been included in this chapter.

The pattern of the beautifully embossed border of the valentine in plate 180 is so fine and unusual that it is a great pleasure to be able to include it here. The background of the medallion is of satin. The dove mounted in the upper portion says: "With thee comes" and the word "Hope" is exquisitely worked out in hand-painted leaves and pasted-on flowers. The hand-colored flowers below have also been applied.

A musical valentine in fine condition is quite a rarity. The one in plate 181, though unmarked, appears to be an Addenbrooke and represents an unusually handsome piece of embossing. The front page lifts lengthwise, to reveal the musical page.

Also rarely encountered are the round valentines in lace. The one. illustrated in plate 182 is in white, gilded. The cupid in the center is a strangely chubby fellow, full of action. The larger wreath which dec-

Plate 178. Embossed valentine with satin center and original envelope.

Plate 179.

Two interesting valentine designs, one by
Dobbs, though unmarked.

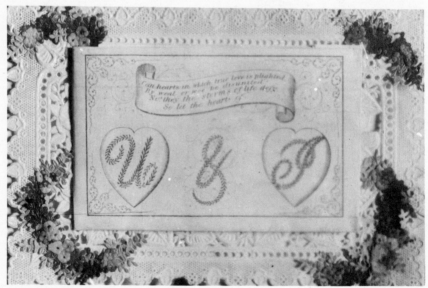

Norcross, New York

Plate 180.

Choice patterns in embossed lace, with satin
background.

orates the lower portion of the valentine consists of silk flowers, for the most part, though a few are in velvet. The small kneeling cupid at the top holds a banner inscribed "Love and Fidelity." This lovely example of valentine art is circa 1875, which is much later than it appears to be.

Flowers so finely painted that at first glance they look like silk embroidery, are incorporated in the French valentine, plate 183. The coloring in the dainty little flowers includes purple, gold, blue, green, and yellow painted on with unusually fine brushes. The valentine is an early one, dating about 1819.

Early paper valentines were frequently decorated with religious subjects, and some of them were utilized for a variety of presentation purposes. This type was prevalent in the Catholic countries of Europe. The English example in plate 184 with lace paper in an all-over pattern of maidenhair fern is especially lovely. The center medallion is beautifully lithographed in fine shades of color. It would appear that the card dates in the 1860's. The inscription at the bottom reads "Wilt thou be mine."

Quite a number of English valentines employed bird feathers as a mode

Plate 181.

A musical valentine.

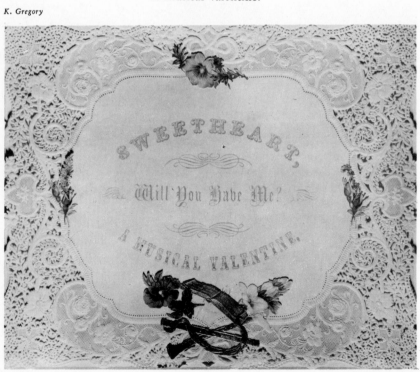

of decoration, for a while during the 1860's, and apparently this novelty proved very popular. Plate 185 displays a typical example. The center is lithographed, and the addition of the feathers completes the lady's attire.

Another amusing novelty of the same period is the valentine adorned with my lady's lace nightcap! The center of the medallion was cut out to

Plate 182.
Attractive round valentine with wreath of
flowers in silk.

allow for the insertion of the cap, complete with satin ribbons. It is inscribed, "Goodnight dear! And in your thoughts forget me not." This may be seen in plate 186.

Plate 187 shows a "dressed" or "paper-doll" valentine. The upper portion and the face of this young lady are in a fine silk velvet, while the

Plate 183.

A French valentine having hand-painted flowers in gay colors, c. 1819.

218

Plate 184.

A religious valentine.

Norcross, New York

Plate 185.

An English valen-
tine decorated with
bird feathers.

219

widely flaring skirt is a novelty print of some sort. The message reads:

"My darling girl
My chosen one,
I dream of you
And you alone."

A group of paper-doll valentines would offer a decided note of interest in any collection. They are, however, quite hard to come by, particularly in fine condition.

No collection would be complete without the inevitable lock of hair! And at least the hair is better off enclosed in a lace-paper envelope on a valentine than in a watch case where the treasure was often confined. More than one jeweler, in the old days, attempted to remove entangled tresses from the works when the owner could not understand why his

Norcross, New York

Plate 186.

Paper-lace valentine with lady's real lace night cap adorning the center.

Plate 187.

"Dressed" or "paper-
doll" valentine.

Plate 188.   Lace envelope containing the inevitable lock of hair.

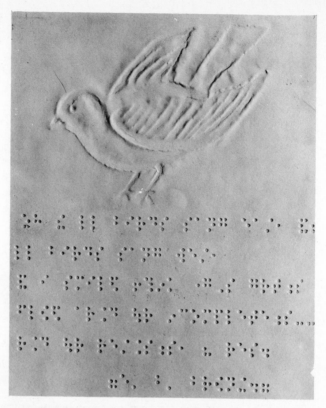

Plate 189.

Valentine in Braille, for the blind.

watch did not run! A lace envelope, a lock of hair, a pink ribbon, and an 1860 suitor's heart beat faster! The sweetheart's lock of hair figured in valentines from the earliest handmades onward down through the years. An example may be seen in plate 188.

It will surprise and please many collectors to know that the blind were not forgotten by the valentine manufacturers. Figures in the way of decoration were embossed in such a way that sensitive fingers could understand them. The Braille valentine shown in plate 189 came from Eltham, Kent and contains quotations from Elizabeth Barrett Browning's "Toll Slowly" and "Rhyme of the Duchess."

As the years passed by, the embossed marks of the various makers gave way to printed names and then finally to trademarks. Still later, some of the American makers, particularly, did not bother to use any mode of identification.

XII

KATE GREENAWAY AND WALTER CRANE

To COLLECTORS OF VALENTINES, Christmas cards, and other items illustrated by Kate Greenaway, the names of Walter Crane and Marcus Ward & Company are closely associated with hers. Walter Crane and Kate Greenaway were both English artists, and both were designing greeting cards for Marcus Ward & Company of Belfast, Ireland, during the years when some of their finest work was accomplished. Though Kate Greenaway did free-lancing before she was fully recognized and made illustrations for other publishers, her most famous cards were produced during her connection with the Marcus Ward Company.

Kate Greenaway was born March 17, 1846 at 1 Cavendish Street, Hoxton. Her father was a wood-engraver and draftsman for *Punch* and also for the *Illustrated London News*. Not a great deal is known about Miss Greenaway's youth except a few relatively unimportant facts. Her legal name was Catherine, hence the "Kate." She lived for a year or two on a farm at Rolleston, then went back to London. After she became established, her studio for years was at Hampstead.

Some of Kate Greenaway's early work was in pen and ink and it was at a "black-and-white" exhibition at the Dudley Gallery in London in 1868, when she was twenty-two years old, that her particular talent was discovered. At least, it is said that recognition came to her through this exhibit when William H. Ward's attention was drawn to her work. The Rev. W. J. Loftie, editor of *The People's Magazine*, also attended this display and purchased her drawings, which depicted sprites, gnomes, and fairies. These were later reproduced from woodcuts in his magazine. In the meantime, Mr. Ward had directed the attention of his firm—Marcus Ward & Company—to Miss Greenaway's talent, as he recognized her special gift in costume figures and dainty colors.

Her first remunerative work was in designing valentines and Christmas cards, but most of these earlier attempts were done anonymously. In the beginning, she made actual models of the Kate Greenaway children in costumes of the late eighteenth century. She achieved her first marked success with a valentine design which she handed to the manager of

Marcus Ward & Company, in London, a new branch of the concern having opened there in 1867. Though the proof was crude and in many ways inharmonious, it had great charm, and as a result, sold 25,000 copies within a few weeks of publication. Despite this, her share of the profit was not more than three pounds, or less than fifteen dollars. She soon turned out several more designs and at the same rate of compensation. However, the Rev. Mr. Loftie, who also had become associated with Marcus Ward & Company, is said to have given her spiritual help and advice which strengthened her career, if not her pocketbook! In fact, he has been prominently identified as having been influential in her early success. In the same category was John Ruskin, reputedly the first to recognize her genius and certainly her greatest champion throughout her life.

Gleeson White, in his *Christmas Cards and Their Chief Designers*, (Studio, Ltd., 1895) remarked that the long series of pictures Kate Greenaway designed for Marcus Ward & Company reflected equal credit on the artist and the concern who produced them. It might be added that the rate of pay she received, at least for her earlier work for this firm, was of no particular credit!

Kate Greenaway's special talent was for the quaint little children she created. She so imbued them with her spirit that they attained a quality which made them wholly hers. Thus she endeared herself and her children for all time. Her coloring, too, had an individual character. In her best-known work she employed pale blue, blue-gray, sage-green, citron, olive, and other shades that were admired by the aesthetic school of decorators of the period.

In examining the Kate Greenaway and Walter Crane cards illustrated in this chapter, it will be noted that they are not as symbolic of Valentine's Day as are earlier or later creations. Indeed, the Kate Greenaway card pictured and signed with the familiar "K. G." signature in plate 190, was also utilized as a Christmas card, the ornament printed in the upper left-hand corner being appropriately changed. Popular basic designs could thus be imprinted for different holidays. This particular card measures 6 by 4 inches. Against a pale blue-gray background, the little girl is pictured in a blue checked cape over a green dress. In one hand she carries a bouquet of flowers, and in the other a blue umbrella. The reverse side of the card has a spray of lilacs and is inscribed, "I bring you some flowers for your valentine." The lower border carries the imprint of "Marcus Ward & Co." Plate 191 pictures a number of Greenaway cards, all of which were published by Marcus Ward, though still others have been found bearing the names of different publishers, including Frederick Ward, Charles Goodall & Sons, as well as Frederick Warne.

It is doubtful if anyone may be certain at this time exactly how many

Plate 190.

Right: Valentine by
Walter Crane.

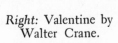

Left: Kate Green-
away valentine.

Author's Collection

225

valentines Kate Greenaway designed over the many years in which she was doing illustrative work. In a volume entitled *The Quiver of Love, A Collection of Valentines, Ancient and Modern,* published by Marcus Ward & Company in 1876, four of her earlier designs are shown. These do not depict children but are of young women, done in a classic, medieval style. These all have a conventional border of leaves and flowers but when issued separately as valentine cards, they have, in addition, a delicately embossed and scalloped edge. On some of the valentines, a greeting or verse is printed on the face of the card, while others carry it on the reverse side. A number of her cards may also be encountered edged with silk fringe, a quaintly Victorian touch.

Kate Greenaway was a versatile artist. Besides her adult figures and her children, she did pastoral scenes, her floral work being quite as graceful and lovely as her children. Much admired also are the scarce "processional" cards in white bas-relief against a plain-colored background, which suggest a distinct Wedgwood feeling. Though Kate Greenaway's children have the greatest appeal for collectors, once an admirer of this beloved English illustrator starts to gather her cards (some of which were made in sets) he seldom specializes. In addition to valentines, Christmas and New Year's cards, her quaint little boys and girls may be found enlivening the pages of storybooks, music books, birthday books, and almanacs, which a collector of her work will seek especially in first editions. Besides *The Quiver of Love* previously mentioned, especially sought after is the first book illustrated by her, entitled *Aunt Louisa's Toy Book.* It was published in 1871 by Frederick Warne & Company, Ltd. of London, the present holder of the bulk of the copyrighted Greenaway work.

It is comparatively seldom that one finds an artist who is really talented in other fields, but Miss Greenaway was fortunate in being additionally gifted as a poetess. Upon completing the illustrations for *Under the Window* she did the accompanying verses. When Edmund Evans, the London color printer, saw the work, he thought so well of it that he sent her on to George Routledge. The publisher was most enthusiastic, and the result was the presentation of *Under the Window* in 1878, which sold seventy thousand copies. There followed, by the same publisher: *The Birthday Book* in 1880; *Mother Goose:* or, *The Old Nursery Rhymes* in 1881; *Little Ann* in 1882; *Language of Flowers* in 1884; *Dame Wiggins of Lee* in 1885; *Marigold Garden* in 1885; and published by George Allen, Sunnyside, Orpington: *The Alphabet Book* about 1885-86. In addition there were her famous almanacs, which she did from 1883 until 1897, with the exception of one for 1896, which was never issued. Other books include *Welcome Manor, A Family Chronicle, The Book of Games, A Day in a Child's Life, Mavors Spelling Book,* and *The Pied Piper of Hamelin.* The last, written by Robert Browning, came out in 1888, not

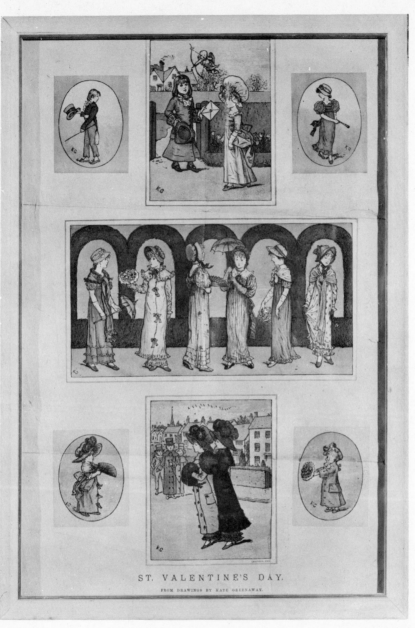

ST. VALENTINE'S DAY.

FROM DRAWINGS BY KATE GREENAWAY.

Plate 191.

Group of Kate Greenaway's children.

227

so many years before her death at the age of fifty-five, on November 6, 1901. Of all her books, *Dame Wiggins of Lee*, with the additional verses by John Ruskin, is one of her best-known works. Little publicity, incidentally, has ever been given to the fact that John Ruskin collected valentines. But when his estate was settled his collection was discovered and sold.

After Kate Greenaway passed away, a book, *Kate Greenaway*, was published in her memory by M. H. Spielmann and G. S. Layard of London in 1905. Fortunate is the owner of a copy of the limited de luxe edition of this volume, which carries an original Greenaway sketch as a frontispiece. The books were signed by her brother, John Greenaway.

Walter Crane was an artist of repute some years before Kate Greenaway appeared on the scene. The four of his valentines which appear in the first edition of *The Quiver of Love* are considered to be the most charming of his printed fanciful designs. The frontispiece in that book carries one of the series, and depicts a romantic-appearing fellow in knee breeches. He is leaning on a fence, apparently making ardent love to a demure-looking maiden attired in a draped gown. When issued as valentines most of these cards are in folder form, edged in paper lace, and with the inside page containing a verse. We find the lines on the second card in this series dedicated to "Spring" by Spenser, the third to "Venus & Cupid" by Spenser (plate 190), while the fourth carries the poem "Cherry Ripe" by Thomas Campion (plate 192). The background of these delightful prints is in a rich gold, and the predominating colors of the designs are medium blues and deep rose-pinks. Border patterns may vary. The strong clean lines of Walter Crane's work are a sheer delight to collectors. As valentines, these cards may be found in more than one size. The smaller one (illustrated here) is 5½ by 4¼ inches, and the larger, 6¾ by 5 inches. They are unsigned. Plate 193 shows another charming design, which has been credited to Crane.

The fact that relatively few valentine or Christmas card designs during the Kate Greenaway-Walter Crane period were seasonal was once noted by *Punch* in London. They lampooned the lightly clad maidens amid spring blossoms, shivering in December sleet!

In England, many of the earliest Christmas cards (the first has been dated from about 1846) as well as some valentines, were created not only by competent artists, but in some instances by famous names. Gleeson White states that Marcus Ward & Company was one of the earliest concerns producing Christmas cards, with a record of the highest level in creative excellence. By reproducing original designs by artists of repute, they commanded all the better class trade. Mr. White has suggested that in the Marcus Ward cards, especially during their middle and later periods, there was a sign of consistent supervision which was largely, if not wholly,

Plate 192.

Choice valentine by
Walter Crane, pub-
lished by Marcus
Ward & Company.

Plate 193.

Rare valentine de-
sign by Walter
Crane.

229

due to the presence of Thomas Crane, director of the firm's department of design. Thomas Crane, Walter's brother, was also an artist. While the general public seemed indifferent to conventional design, he upheld the high standards of the concern, and was responsible for a series of new cards notable not only for the excellence of their pictures, or floral devices, but for the subdued and appropriate ornamentation on their borders and backs.

Many of the greeting cards of this period were made as folding cards. Representing four cards in one, they were of course more expensive to produce—and to purchase. Plate 194 shows a card of this type. The stylized pattern is white on a yellow background, while the graceful figures in the pasted-on medallions are exquisite pastel-colored lithographs. The embossed border is striped and delicately touched with gold. On the inside of the folder are two scenes, one depicting autumn and the other winter. Each contains a verse, heavily edged with a band of gold. One is entitled "Love" by Thomas Hood, and the other, "Love's Invitation," is taken from Shakespeare. This card might be considered a typical Marcus Ward valentine of the period, if indeed any card during such a highly commercialized era can be thus termed.

To presume to present a complete picture of the thousands of cards produced by Marcus Ward Company would be an impossibility. However, collectors specializing in old greeting cards soon learn to distinguish the Kate Greenaway cards, often carrying the familiar "K. G." signature; the valentines designed by Walter Crane, which are unsigned; and the general style and coloring of the work done by Marcus Ward & Company, with their identifying "Marcus Ward & Co." printed in small type. It requires an experienced collector to detect the *unsigned* Kate Greenaway cards but these add zest to the joy of collecting. American scrapbooks are often found containing advertising cards, some in a style so similar to Kate Greenaway's that they deceive the unwary, particularly when the advertising material has been cut away.

Louis Prang of Boston was the equivalent of London's Marcus Ward, in the greeting-card business. It was Prang who specialized in chromolithography. While he published many Christmas, New Year's, and Easter cards, his valentines were in the minority. Many of them were small and the coloring so delicate as to border on the anemic. Three of his best, as taken from one of his sample books, are illustrated here for comparison with his contemporaries. His subjects were generally either flowers or naked cupids, but there were exceptions. One of his cupids is shown in plate 195, and other examples, as described in chapter III, in plates 196 and 197. Collectors would do well to add any worth-while Prang specimens to their collection.

Kate Greenaway's passing at the turn of the century almost seemed

Plate 194.

A folding valentine card by Marcus Ward & Company.

Plate 195.

Valentine by Louis Prang, of Boston, dated 1893.

Plate 196.

A tomato valentine, from days when they were ornaments and called "love apples," dated 1888.

231

Plate 197. A valentine by Louis Prang, Boston, in style of Kate Greenaway, dated 1882.

to spell a death-knell for the popularity of the finer English greeting cards. It has been said that Messrs. De la Rue and Marcus Ward were outstanding as "classical" publishers, who withstood demand for any sort of novelty at a price. However, credit must also be accorded Raphael Tuck & Company, S. Hildesheimer & Company, and Hildesheimer & Faulkner, as publishers of enormous quantities of excellent cards. By the early 1900's the English could not meet the competition offered here by the cheaper German imports since these were lithographed cards as against the more expensive stone process used by the English. The market in the Old World, furthermore, was flooded with the chromolithographs perfected by Prang of Boston, whose different subjects proved to be distinctly more up to date than most offered by their own firms. What the English desired was a new era of appreciation of their traditional designs and methods of manufacture, but times had changed.

LIST OF AMERICAN VALENTINE PUBLISHERS

In each instance the years they are known to have been in business are given. The dates cannot be entirely accurate, since some makers were doubtless earlier or later than recorded, and several moved their location many times.

American Valentine Company, 165 William Street and 14 Chambers Street, New York, 1860's.
   In 1863 advertised "Soldier's valentine packets, Army valentine packets, Torch of Love, New Military comic valentine, New Musical comic valentines," etc.

Thomas Barby, London and Philadelphia, 1780 and possibly in early 1800's.

Berlin, also Berlin & Jones (Jacob Berlin), New York, Stationer, 1850–1851; West & Berlin, 1854–1855; Henry Berlin & George H. Jones, 1859–1869.

Bullard Art Publishing Company, 492 Main Street, Worcester, Mass., removed to Springfield, Mass., 1887–1888.

Philip J. Cozans (later Huestis & Cozans), New York, 1850–1862.

Pasqual Donaldson, 178 Orchard Street, New York, 1839–1855.
   First name sometimes spelled "Pascal."

George Dunn & Company, Richmond, Va., 1860's.
   Publishers, probably few valentines.

Elton (Robert H.) & Company, New York, 1833–1855.
   Claimed to have published valentines as early as 1834.
   Sold out to McLoughlin Brothers.

Abraham Fisher (born 1812), Philadelphia and New York, 1836–1860.
   Fisher & Brothers
   Fisher & E. G.
   Fisher & Dennison
   A. J. Fisher
   Published Valentine Writer, 1840.

   Philadelphia:
      Turner & Fisher
      Fisher & Brothers
   Sold out to George C. Whitney, Worcester, Mass.

T. Frere, 83 Nassau Street, New York, 1852–1855.

G. S. Haskins & Company, 36 Beekman Street, New York, 1861–1863.
Valentine packages and valentines for soldiers. Many varieties for the army.
May have been a jobber.

J. R. Hawley & Company, 165 William Street, New York.
May have been a jobber.

Benjamin W. Hitchcock, 455 Broadway, New York.
Valentines to the trade by mail. Store and manufactory.

Esther Howland, 16 Summer Street and 425 Main Street, Worcester, Mass.,
1849–1881.
Also, New England Valentine Company

Charles P. Huestis, 104 Nassau Street, corner Ann., New York, 1841-1853.
Charles Robb & Huestis (see also Cozans)

Hunter & Company, Hinsdale, N. H., 1858.

McLoughlin Brothers, New York, removed to Springfield, Mass., 1940; 1848–
1950.

Charles Magnus, 12 Frankfort Street, New York, 1854–1870.

Richard Marsh, New York, 1850–1854.
Published valentine bank notes.

David W. Moody, 140 Nassau Street, New York, listed as lithographer for one
year, 1846; 128 Fulton Street, draughtsman, 1849.

New England Valentine Company, Esther Howland, 16 Summer Street and
425 Main Street, Worcester, Mass., 1870 (?)–1881.

New York Union Valentine Company, 134 Williiam Street, New York.

New York Valentine Corner, 134 William Street, New York.

Louis Prang, Boston and Roxbury, Mass., 1867–1889.

George Snyder, began at 112 John Street, New York, as lithographer, 1845;
122 Fulton Street, 1846–1847; 138 William Street, 1848–1850; 87 Fulton Street, 1852; 92 William Street, 1857–1892.

T. W. Strong, 153 Fulton Street and 98 Nassau Street, New York, 1842–1869.

Jotham Taft, Worcester, Mass., 1863–1889.
Son, Edward Taft, 1879–1880. (Record obscure but he worked in valentines
before 1879.)

Fred Turner, Philadelphia, 1843–1850.
Turner and Fisher, 1843–1849
Also 74 Chatham Street (see Fisher)

Edward A. Whaites, 1 Courthan Street and 347 Broadway, New York, 1836–
1868.

George C. Whitney Company, Whitney Brothers, Whitney Manufacturing
Company, Worcester, Mass., 1866–1942.

James Wrigley, 27 Chatham Street, New York, 1846–1870.

INDEX

* See Color Supplement between pages 106 and 107.

* *See Color Supplement between pages 106 and 107.*

Whatman, J., 135
White, Gleeson, 224, 228
Whitney, Edward, 67
Whitney, Edward C., 68
Whitney, George C., 67, 80, 138, 196
   attitude of, toward comics, 71
Whitney, George C., & Company, 64,
    66, 67-75
   burning of building, 72, 74
   growth of business of, 71-72
   identification marks used by, 68
   prices of valentines, 75
   verse department of, 72

Whitney, Lura Clark, 67
Whitney, Sumner, 67
Whitney, Warren A., 75
Windsor, John, 181, 184, 185, 186,
   187, 188
women employees, see girls
Wood, S. T., 95, 194, 199
Wood, Thomas, 194, 196, 199
woodcuts, 39
World War I valentine, 105
World War II valentine, 105
Wrigley, James, comic valentines of,
   82, 83

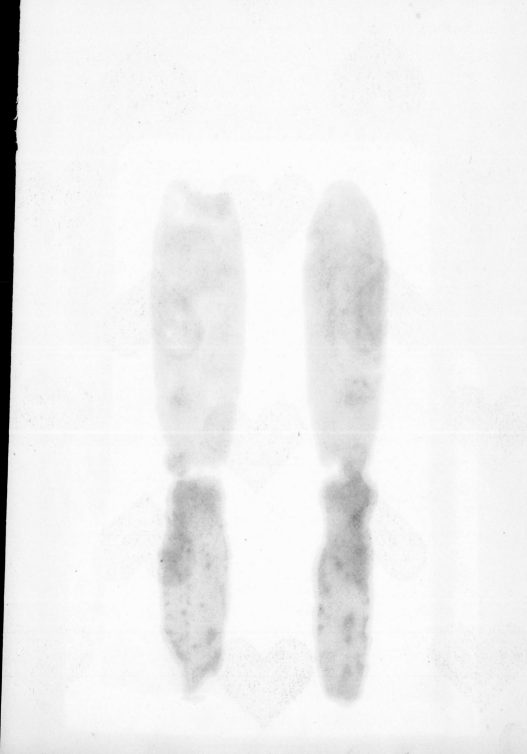